Approaching Youth Studies

Approaching Youth Studies

Being, Becoming, and Belonging

Kate Tilleczek

OXFORD
UNIVERSITY PRESS

OXFORD
UNIVERSITY PRESS

8 Sampson Mews, Suite 204, Don Mills, Ontario M3C 0H5
www.oupcanada.com

Oxford University Press is a department of the University of Oxford.
It furthers the University's objective of excellence in research, scholarship,
and education by publishing worldwide in

Oxford   New York

Auckland   Cape Town   Dar es Salaam   Hong Kong   Karachi
Kuala Lumpur   Madrid   Melbourne   Mexico City   Nairobi
New Delhi   Shanghai   Taipei   Toronto

With offices in

Argentina   Austria   Brazil   Chile   Czech Republic   France   Greece
Guatemala   Hungary   Italy   Japan   Poland   Portugal   Singapore
South Korea   Switzerland   Thailand   Turkey   Ukraine   Vietnam

Oxford is a trade mark of Oxford University Press
in the UK and in certain other countries

Published in Canada
by Oxford University Press

Library and Archives Canada Cataloguing in Publication
Tilleczek, Kate C. (Kate Clare), 1963–
Approaching youth studies: being, becoming, belonging / Kate Tilleczek.
Includes bibliographical references and index.
ISBN 978-0-19-542763-9

1. Youth—Study and teaching—Textbooks. 2. Youth—Research—Textbooks.
I. Title.

HQ796.T56 2010   305.235072   C2010-904304

Cover image: Ozgurdonmaz/iStockphoto

Oxford University Press is committed to our environment. This book is printed on
Forest Stewardship Council certified paper, harvested from a responsibly managed forest.

Mixed Sources
Product group from well-managed
forests and other controlled sources
www.fsc.org Cert no. SW-COC-000952
© 1996 Forest Stewardship Council

Printed and bound in Canada

1 2 3 4 — 14 13 12 11

CONTENTS

Chapter 8 Action, Practice, and Policy *with* and *for* Youth   128

ACKNOWLEDGEMENTS

Writing is difficult and joyful; it makes for a certain way of living. Fortunate is the one who has many teachers and shoulders to weep upon. This book is dedicated to my dearest Ron with whom I have the enjoyment of sharing this ponderous form of life. He has the broadest shoulders I have ever seen. It is also dedicated to our sons, William and Elliott (and all of their friends), the finest young people I know. These guys know how to live and write; they have taught me so very much.

Words are not enough to express my thanks to Ellen, Judy, Robin, Anne, Tom, and Mark, with whom I shared our youth, stories, and music. I would not have wanted it any other way. My nieces and nephews continue to inspire me. Thanks to Jennifer, Ellen, Elizabeth, Emily, Carey, Alex, Charlotte, and Olivia. You guys rock. And this book is for Bebhinn and William for teaching us all how to read, write, think, love, and educate.

A special gratitude is expressed to my colleagues in the Community Health Systems Group at the Hospital for Sick Children in Toronto, especially to my colleagues/mentors/friends Bruce Ferguson, Katherine Boydell, Anneke Rummens, and Dara Roth Edney. In addition, the fine people at Oxford University Press were the perfect blend of competent and supportive, especially Andrea Kennedy.

INTRODUCTION

Approaching Youth Studies: Being, Becoming, Belonging is about the lives and times of young people and the ways in which youth have been studied and understood. This book addresses a range of young people's contexts and experiences in contemporary society and is an overview of the field of youth studies for those who research, live, and work with young people. As opposed to research *about* youth, *Approaching Youth Studies* is about how we might work *with* and *for* young people. I have written this text from my current position as a parent of teenagers, as an educator, and as a university professor and researcher who strives to assist young people through their various transitions and struggles.

As Griffen (1997) and others have duly noted, the field of youth studies is in flux. This fluctuation is one focus of this book; the other is to provide a current and critical examination of the research, practice, and policies relating to young people. The book presents information about the lives and contexts of youth and suggests ways to ask and answer the questions we have about young people and ways to include them in the process. It invites readers into an ongoing conversation about what it is to study young people and how best to do it. The book is, therefore, selective of research and practices that illustrate young people's negotiations, challenges, and successes. *Approaching Youth Studies: Being, Becoming, Belonging* is dedicated to understanding and bettering the lives of young people through work *with*, *for*, and *by* them.

There are both challenges and fortunes found in the study of youth. On the one hand, many scholars consider nuances of social theory and methods to detail possibilities and problems of living as a young person. These will be reviewed here. On the other hand, those who work with or govern young people remain ill-informed about the emergence of this work and of youth studies more generally. For instance, the idea that all youth are the same and are necessarily deviant has been challenged on many grounds but continues to reverberate in a good deal of media, policy, and practice.

Canadians currently bear witness to squabbles over the federal plan to change the age of majority, provincial plans to tie driving privileges to school completion, ongoing discussions about the age at which juvenile and adult justice converge, and community debates relating to setting curfews for youth. The profusion of experiences and cultural contexts is being studied, but polices and programs that govern the lives of young people in schools, in communities, on the roads, in the health system, and so forth, do not act on evidence. The history of these debates and ideas about youth form another focus of the book: tensions and myths about young people are examined to form a current conversation about youth studies.

The book is being written following the inauguration of Barack Obama as the president of the United States and during a large-scale economic crisis. Canadian and global media are awash in festivities and speculations and quick to point out both a doom-filled picture of society and the youth-friendly nature of the inaugural events and, so-far, the presidency. Rock stars such as Bono, will.i.am, Beyoncé, and Bruce Springsteen performed at one massive public inaugural event to remind viewers that this president is reaching out to young people and to the vitality, energy, and idea of youth. The predictions are that the Millennium Generation (those youth born in the 1990s and through the turn of the century) will dictate US policy in the near future. We shall see.

The social and political inclusion or exclusion of young people is an important development to track in the coming years. Young people are the divining rods and tropical frogs of the bell jars of modern society. Their lives and experiences indicate a convergence of the social, political, economic, and experiential centres of modern life. At the very time that young people are actively negotiating this modern world, their elders are taking up a complex and contradictory stance on youth. This stance tends to take the form of an appropriation of youth and 'being young' and an unmistakable clamour to look and act youthful. An increasing number of plastic surgeries, health supplements, diet and exercise regimens, beauty products, and sexual function medications are consumed in an insatiable demand to remain young. At the same time, we are marginalizing actual young people and creating a climate of increased dependence. Latham (2002) pointedly refers to this irony as 'consuming youth'. He shows the competing tensions of the lives of modern young people by invoking the metaphors of vampires and cyborgs. This book unpacks these ideas and examines digital and consumer contexts as important in this regard.

These and other social events in the lives and experiences of youth must be examined while young people attempt to actively negotiate them. Furlong and Cartmel (2007) have aptly summarized important shifts in political, economic, and social contexts as those encompassing a host of economic and labour market alterations that influence schools, places of work, homes, leisure activities, and peer relations. *Approaching Youth Studies: Being, Becoming, Belonging* examines the data relating to these changes in the lives of young people, including the place of modern technological changes and the theories, methods, and practices that have arisen in youth studies.

As such, the book presents a cautiously optimistic view of young people and of the field of youth studies. It draws upon research evidence and theory across disciplines of sociology, anthropology, history, cultural studies, psychology, philosophy, health, and education in answering questions and examining contexts. Once the nearly exclusive domain of psychology and biology, youth studies is becoming attuned to insights from many disciplines. The field could be further pushed to become a social science *with* and *for* young people. This kind of youth studies suggests new ways to examine the roots and experiences of social inequalities and the daily experiences of them (cf. Cohen, 1996; Cohen & Ainley, 2000; Côté & Allahar, 2006).

In summary, the book approaches youth studies in contemporary contexts and provides evidence and analysis on the most critical and interesting debates and issues in the field. The book aims to examine and understand the myths under which society operates in relation to its young people. It undertakes to make plain the use of the term *culture* as applied to young people and focuses on stratifications along ethnic, social class, region, gender, sexuality, and age lines. In particular, the text argues for consideration of youth studies *with*, *for*, and *by* young people.

In so doing, Chapter 1 addresses a general approach for youth studies and also addresses reverberating themes: being, becoming, and belonging as fundamental social processes that have repeatedly emerged. Chapter 2 explores some myths of youth studies and places the concept of youth in a brief social historical and cultural context. This chapter argues that youth occupy an often precarious position on the margins of society and should be understood and treated in new ways. Chapters 3 and 4 continue this discussion by investigating ways to ask and answer outstanding questions about the lives and experiences of young people. These chapters draw together insights from a selection of theories, practices, and methods currently applied to youth. The chapters also pose a challenge to imagine a social science *with* and *for* young people rather than one that simply describes, pathologizes, or treats young people as a discourse.

Next, Chapter 5 provides a modern context for work and play, leisure and labour, and provides philosophical consideration of the impacts of technology on experience. This chapter provides a solid point of entry into debates about technology and consumer society as they intrude on youth. The blurring of lines between work and leisure and the modern character of each are discussed. Chapter 6 places young people at their intersections of modern schools, families, friends, and communities. The research described is that which is most in-tune with the emerging field of youth studies. While Canadian in focus, the synthesis also draws on international scholarship and that which attempts to examine complexities of contexts at multiple cultural levels. The work examines cultural contexts, nests, experiences, and transitions in the bright light.

The final chapters connect this evidence and theory to a summary discussion of the daily experiences of youth. Chapter 7 does so through careful consideration of identity and debates relating to risk and resiliency. Chapter 8 concludes the book by considering Canadian and international programs, policies, and practices from diverse fields, such as mental health, education, and international human rights. The chapter provides a means by which to scrutinize the social treatment of youth as currently carried out by politicians, policy makers, and practitioners. It ends with a consideration of social action by young people and a summary of the book's arguments and directions for youth studies.

Part One

The Fountains and Follies of Youth: Conceptualizing Youth Studies

The first two chapters in the book outline a new approach to youth studies as grounded in theories and evidence of the past. This section of the book refers to the 'fountains and follies' of youth in an attempt to trace how society has viewed youth. In the first case, the fountain of youth refers to society's ongoing attempts to remain young. Throughout the ages, adults have tried to stave off inevitable decline. On the other hand, young people themselves have not been well treated or conceived of. Such promises and problems of youth are a main theme of the first two chapters of this book.

Specifically, Chapter 1 will posit a complex cultural nesting approach to youth studies as a new way to address these problems and promises. Three foundational social processes are suggested in youth studies, which drive the complex cultural nesting approach: *being*, *becoming*, and *belonging*. Chapter 1 demonstrates how this approach illuminates the liminality of modern youth, their experiences, and the social, political, and historical contexts that organize them. Also discussed are three preoccupations of youth studies: culture, development, and praxis; a current example of this approach is provided vis-à-vis narrative testimonials from young people.

Chapter 2 proceeds to map out some historical and mythic foundations for youth studies and discuss three myths: (1) the epistemological fallacy of modern society; (2) the myth that youth is necessarily risky, stormy, and stressful; and (3) the myth that our current notions of youth have always been with us. This chapter sketches the socio-historic influences that impinge upon youth and with which youth interact and actively negotiate; the chapter also provides a brief and critical social history of youth studies. This section of the book ends with 10 critical reflections on youth studies as presented in Chapters 1 and 2.

Chapter One

Toward Contemporary Youth Studies

I am not arguing that we are seeing a simplistic 'march of progress' forwards into a newly enlightened approach to work with young people or representations of their lives, but it is important to recognise . . . that it is no longer possible to write or talk about 'youth' in precisely the same terms as twenty, even ten years ago. (Griffen, 1997)

The current compilation of structural inequalities, and the forms of self-narration through which they are actively contested and reproduced, clearly requires more sophisticated and empirically grounded accounts than this. If we are to do justice to what is at stake for young people's lives, we have to find new ways of integrating empirically grounded and dialogical strategies of youth research within interdisciplinary and theoretically sophisticated frameworks of comparative analysis. (Cohen & Ainley, 2000: 242)

Introduction

Young people of today are very much situated within modern society. Much has been written about elements of consumption, fear, individualism, rationality, and the loss of a spirited eros in modern technological cultures (Srigley, forthcoming). But current knowledge has yet to provide a true rendering of how youth experiences are socially organized by modern society's institutions, such as schools, governments, families, and labour markets. Rather than simply restating that poverty and/or ethnicity matter in creating experiences and inequalities for youth, the meaning and entrenchment of these experiences and inequalities require investigation. This kind of analysis is, in fact, underway in Europe, where researchers address the need for transnational, social, philosophical, and historical considerations of youth (Cohen, 1999; Chisholm, 2006) and are showing how experiences and treatment of young people shift with these modern social and political realities (Furlong & Cartmel, 2007; James

& Prout, 2001). This chapter begins by suggesting an approach to youth studies that makes room for such analysis. Later in the chapter, some of the findings from the *Early School Leavers Project* are shared to explicate the approach.

A Starting Point: Toward Complex Cultural Nests

There are two pressing questions in youth studies: (1) To what extent are youth experiences influenced by modern society? (2) How do these influences work? Out of these two questions, however, spring a whole host of other important questions to consider: What does this mean for the treatment of the young in society? How do young people find their way? How do they act, resist, conform, and negotiate their social contexts? What are the fundamental social processes by which they do so? Can we help them to craft good lives?

Evidently, being a young person and becoming an adult can be both filled with joy and fraught with challenges. Attending to contexts surrounding transitional points is a good way to observe and understand those transitions. Cohen (1999), however, makes a fine point about the downfalls of 'youth-as-transition' approaches that focus on individual and linear pathways. In my own youth studies research, I also argue that it is neither useful nor necessary to conceptualize transitions in a simplistic one-directional fashion with the finding of a good job as the final and only measure of success in life. Instead, I posit a *complex cultural nesting approach* as an interpretive framework that offers a means of studying precisely the ways in which youth experiences are nonlinear and occur in social contexts that are nested inside one another.

The concept of a nest is applied in two ways. A nest refers to the need for homey comfort and evokes a sense of belonging. For young people, belonging occurs in schools, in homes, with friends, in communities, etc. (see Figure 1.1). Nests also suggest that contexts can be stacked up, or nested within one another, each offering different but simultaneous experiences. A young person's biography therefore co-occurs at numerous levels. This approach is further elaborated in the book but is introduced here to provide a starting place to discuss youth studies. The approach is offered for criticism and scrutiny in illuminating youth research and practice.

The complex cultural nesting approach has come from my work over two decades. This approach facilitates investigations of young people's experiences and movements through the vast number of changing social contexts in which they find themselves—such as schools, health-care settings, politics, labour markets, digital contexts, families, and communities. Such investigations focus upon inequities and their entrenchments in youth lives across the many transitions they make (e.g., moving from elementary to secondary school, encountering mass media and technology, learning to drive, going to work). Investigations also compare local contexts with global and historical work. The

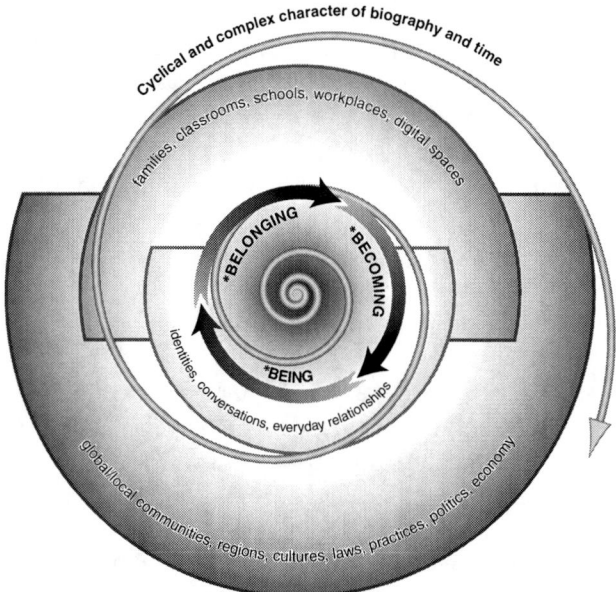

*Represents three fundamental social process of youth development (across social, emotional,
physical and psychological dimensions). Each occurs within nested social contexts.

Figure 1.1 Complex Cultural Nests

approach shifts away from simple, linear, 'at-risk' characterizations of young people toward moments of resourcefulness of youth and of those closest to them (parents, educators, health-care professionals, friends). Our studies of inequalities relating to race, ethnicity, gender, age, and social class and their impacts on youth are therefore more nuanced in that they attend to similarities and differences in contexts and across time.

Young people and those closest to them are inseparable from their cultures and are nested within many social contexts at any moment. Urie Bronfenbrenner (2005, 1979) has produced the most important work for describing the multiple levels at which various nested influences occur. These levels of concentric systems—microsystem, mesosystem, macrosystem, and chronosystem—are well known to researchers and practitioners who assist youth in negotiating their way through life. The levels of *micro, meso, macro,* and *chrono* are therefore adapted from Bronfenbrenner's (1979) *The Ecology of Human Development,* which describes the different social environments that influence youth.

A *microsystem* is a pattern of activities, roles, and interpersonal relations that young people experience in a given setting with particular physical and material characteristics. Such a setting is a place where young people readily engage in face-to-face interactions; some examples are homes, part-time workplaces, the schoolyard, and the classroom. A young person is involved in several different microsystems at once, including family, school, and friendships, each presenting different relationships and institutions to be negotiated; therefore, parents, teachers, coaches, friends, classmates, siblings, step-parents, and grandparents are of significance and the interrelation between them is important. Notions of self, identity, and a community of beings belong to microsystems even though they also exist at all levels. The microsystem can be thought of, then, as the heart of the model given the day-to-day, intimate character of the interactions among many social beings. These social relationships and community of beings occupy centre stage.

The term *mesosystem* refers to the interrelations among people in two or more settings in which the young person *actively* participates (for example, the relations among home, school, neighbourhood, peer group). The idea of the active young person is a theoretically important one (James & Prout, 2001; Jenks, 1996) since it allows for the ways in which youth negotiate with, advocate for, make changes to, and react to environments. A mesosystem is, thus, 'a system of microsystems' (Bronfenbrenner, 1979, p. 25). Mesosystem relations have a bearing (although not always directly) on young people's lives. For example, if parents have had a terrible time with their own schooling experiences and therefore react negatively to their child's current teachers, the young person is implicated.

In the complex cultural nesting approach, the meso level houses liminal areas—those between cultures and individuals. This is the space from which we can appreciate intersections and practices in daily lives of young people as they live them within their community of beings. It is here that the experience and embodiment of social class, poverty, ethnicity, identity, and age are played out and form a crux of cultural nests (Tilleczek, 2007b). Such areas of liminality form a focus of this approach. For example, in our recent study of youth transition from elementary to secondary school (Tilleczek et al., 2009), it was the interplay between young people's notion of being richer or poorer than their classmates that influenced their adjustments to school. The liminal area of the classroom, then, gathered macro-level issues (poverty and social class) and micro-level issues (sense of self and identity) together.

The *macrosystem* refers to patterns, consistencies, and inconsistencies in the form and content of micro and meso systems. The macrosystem describes processes at the level of society and culture, including the enacting of political governance, laws, beliefs, practices, values, and ideologies. Some of the events that influence young people are not attributable to their immediate environment but are characteristic of larger global, regional, or national social contexts. Examples include the processes of globalization; large-scale political or economic factors, such as poverty, recession, and educational policy; and historical trends in views about young people.

In addition, the complex cultural nesting approach to youth studies acknowledges the importance of the *chronosystem*—the timing and patterning

Box 1.1 Seeing Cultural Nests

In order to further concretize the complex cultural nesting approach, an additional figure is presented here from the important work of the Canadian Council on Learning (CCL). The CCL has collectively developed three models of holistic and lifelong learning based on First Nation, Metis, and Inuit ways of knowing. While not precisely identical to the complex cultural nesting approach, the First Nation's model is a fine visual example of work currently underway to approach the promises and problems encountered by Aboriginal youth in educational systems. The model sketches out the complex meanings of learning/education as embedded in layers of contexts over the life course and provides a means for discussing alternate ways in which education/learning can be imagined rather than simple, linear, momentary 'achievement' models. To see an interactive model of the figure, go to www.ccl-cca.ca/CCL/Reports/RedefiningSuccessInAboriginalLearning/RedefiningSuccessPartners.html.

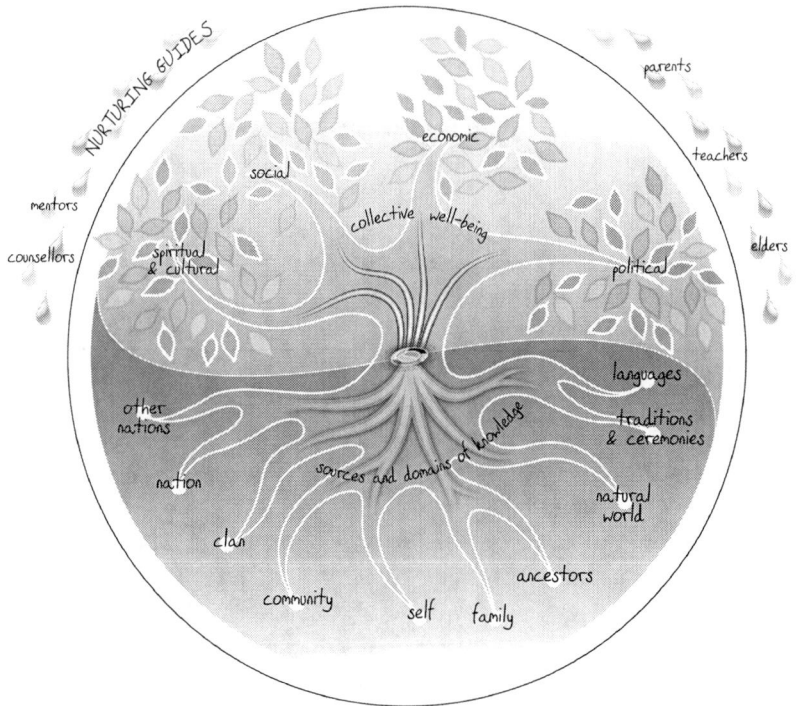

Figure 1.2 Complex Cultural Nesting Approach

of lives. The *chronosystem* reminds us that individuals and/or groups of young people live in position to historical time and its developments and suggests the critical character of history in understanding young people. Glen Elder's important work on children in time and place is one such example wherein the influences of war and economic depression on the long-term life trajectories of young people were examined. Indeed, the inclusion of this kind of long-term and cross-time research is integral to youth studies.

Bronfenbrenner's bio-ecological model also suggests that young people making transitions—for example, from elementary to secondary school—confront an 'ecological transition' (p. 26) since they are adapting to role and setting changes that can impede or facilitate in many ways. Bronfenbrenner also reminds us that 'every ecological transition is both a consequence and an instigator of developmental processes' (p. 27), and he has summarized a theoretical direction that has shaped a generation of subsequent research, including the approach outlined here.

The ecology of human development was said to involve the 'scientific study of progressive, mutual accommodations between an active, growing human being and the changing properties of the immediate settings' (p. 21) in which a young person lives. To this I add the importance of also examining the relationships and social relations in these settings, which are themselves socially and politically constituted. The young person is always a social young person and youth studies examines what it means to understand these interconnecting and nested social relations.

The complex cultural nesting approach reminds us of these complex levels and settings. But it also addresses the fundamental social processes (*being, becoming,* and *belonging*) by which these contexts hold and distribute opportunities or constraints. As well, the complex cultural nesting approach provides a way to investigate and interrogate the social organization of daily experiences across these various levels of influences. Many theories and models from disciplines across social sciences and humanities have informed the complex cultural nesting approach, including contextual meta-models such as Lerner's (2002) developmental contextual model, Elder's (1995) life course theory, and forms of indigenous knowledge (Canadian Council on Learning, 2007; Smith, 2004). The approach is not conventionally 'developmental'. It provides a critical root description of fundamental social processes and includes culture as an indispensable concept because of its ability to influence (and be influenced by) actions and to shape the habits and skills from which young people, families, and educators construct strategies for daily action (Swidler, 1986). There are primarily three preoccupations of note in the complex cultural nesting approach.

The first preoccupation in this approach is culture, which is a crucial idea in understanding young people and yet remains a contested concept with variable definitions. It is used here to represent both material and nonmaterial aspects of the lives of young people as found across the four systems outlined above (macro, meso, macro, and chrono). Material aspects of culture are the myriad tangible artifacts that can be examined, such as cellphones, iPods, Game Boys, school policies on bullying, blue jeans, nose rings, tattoos, movies, state laws on young offenders, and correctional facilities. Nonmaterial aspects of culture concern the societal representations, values, attitudes, and ideas about such things as youth, education, families, punishment, or the importance of technology. These ideas and assumptions shape the logic of practice in prevention, policy, programs, and treatment of young people. For instance, how is it that our society organizes the four systems and sets up the social relations that govern youth?

If culture is a primary preoccupation in contemporary youth studies, development is a close second. As stated earlier, the complex cultural nesting approach is not developmental in the traditional sense where young people move along easily and in step-wise, determined linear pathways. But time and maturation (physical, emotional, social, and cognitive) do remain central aspects, albeit conceived in nonlinear ways and nested within social contexts and cultures. Such attention to nonprogressive and nonlinear notions of development allow for understanding of how and why young people live out their complex biographies and what they may do when encountering risk or resiliency situations (Unger, 2008; Pais, 2003). The preoccupation with a nonlinear development places a focus of study on the tensions between stability and change, sameness and difference in development of young people over time. The model leaves room for examining positive experiences and recovery from troubling situations. Youths' lives are characterized by any number of pathways that intersect along levels of influence in schools, communities, and societies. For example, schools do not stand alone but are nested in social and political contexts of power and hold numerous contradictions (Bruner, 1996; Tilleczek, 2008d). The model urges us to avoid seeing all members of risk groups (e.g., youth living in poverty) as necessarily at risk without also seeing *how* they have been put in risk situations and their real potential for acting on situations of resilience (Unger, 2004). In the best of this work, problems are not simply individualized but are seen as distributed in social contexts in which young people can act and resist as well as conform.

The third and final preoccupation of the complex cultural nesting approach is that the theories and understanding about youth cannot be separated from the way society treats them (practice). Practice includes such endeavours as participating in political action, teaching, doing research, writing policy, or nursing someone to health. The idea of *praxis* suggests that theory and practice become inseparable, and calls for sensible relevance of our knowledge about young people. *Praxis* has been defined as 'the practical application of any type of learning or idea'; or 'a process by which a theory, lesson or skill is enacted or practiced'; or 'a complex activity by which individuals create culture and society, and become critically conscious human beings by comprising a cycle of action-reflection-action . . . ' (Educate Magazine, 2009). In Chapter 3, *praxis* is further described as relating to forms of social inquiry.

In the cultural nesting approach, theory and research are conducted as praxis for understanding lives and enhancing social practices. A continuous loop of knowledge-making and discussion is built into the design, methods, and strategies of research. Currents arising from such places as subaltern studies (cf. Apple & Buras, 2006), critical 'praxicological' social inquiry (Carroll, 2004), institutional ethnography (Smith, 2002) and voiced research (cf. Smyth & Hattam, 2001) are adapted so as to speak to, listen to, and hear young people. The issues of how we ask and answer our questions about young people (theory, method, and praxis) will be exemplified in Chapters 3 and 4.

Being, Becoming, and Belonging

In reading and working within the fields of youth studies over two decades, I have found much of the scholarship to encompass tensions between *being* young and *becoming* older. Research and writing in the area tends to focus on the latter; the former is more nominal and less well understood. In addition, the critical and necessary need for young people to find a fit in their social surroundings recurs in the need for enhanced *belonging*. I have found abundant works of art that represent youth in this manner and assist in illustrating these tensions, in works as diverse as Caravaggio's *Youth Bitten by a Green Lizard* (1592–93) from the Italian Baroque, to Munch's *Puberty* (1894) from German expressionism, to contemporary Canadian portraiture such as Marianna Gartner's incredible depictions of the tensions of children and youth in *Girl with Siamese Twins* (2007). These paintings capture transitional visions and experiences of liminal spaces between childhood and adulthood in which critical social passages and experiences happen. So frequent are themes of being, becoming, and belonging discussed in youth studies that I suggest they are among the fundamental social processes underlying development.

For instance, tensions exist for youth between the self and other; between friends and enemies; between future, past, and present; between emotional drama and calm; and between stability and change. Young people live their everyday lives, just *being* who they are now. But they are always in the process of (and constantly reminded about) becoming the people they will be. They feel, experience, react, and negotiate their place and intersecting identities within families, schools, political systems, friendships, and communities, all the while becoming their more biologically mature selves. Bodies are inhabited in new ways as puberty alters them and society responds, and puberty is not to be divided from its social implications. Young people are 'being and becoming in their bodies' (Tilleczek, 2009) in ways that will be elaborated upon in greater detail through this book.

Being and *becoming* have long histories in philosophy, literature, art, and social science, and although a detailed discussion of this is not within the scope of this book, a brief consideration of these terms in western philosophy and social science is useful. In the most obvious sense, young people are in simultaneous and constant motion between being and becoming. Not the least of these tensions are those that occur in the process of *being* oneself in everyday life. This lived experience consists of living in the moment of time and living outside or across time into the future. Young people forge identities through daily negotiations at school, home, community, work, and with friends. As such, they need to be valued for who they are *now*. They require places to simply be and belong. However, young people are also in a state of *becoming* young adults while moving across and through contexts and institutions. They are changing physically, emotionally, and intellectually. Understanding these complex processes of change and stability over time and across nested transitions is necessary to gain a window into becoming. We are able to capture such tensions in stories, tales, biographies, and narratives.

Stories show us the tensions that exist in the realm of being, in the pathways to becoming, and in the tensions experienced between them. For example, a young Aboriginal girl who must leave her home, family, and community to attend a high school will embody multiple tensions of being and becoming. Her transition to high school varies from that of the young people in her new school who happened to have grown up around the block from the school and are part of dominant non-Aboriginal culture. Much has been written about the power of stories, paintings, narratives biographies, etc., to render true descriptions and understandings about life when other words are woefully inadequate. The intricacy of such art-informed and narrative modes of inquiry is explored in Chapters 4 and 7 to examine biographies of young people and to interpret the stories they tell.

Besides their narrative charm, the concepts of being and becoming are also related to other currents in youth studies. For example, Chapter 7 details and critiques the much discussed and debated ideas of risk and resilience. It is useful to be aware that the label of youth 'at risk' abounds in this field. But young people should better be seen as *living in* risk situations, rather than as containers *of risk*. Risk statuses also fluctuate over time and are contingent on circumstance in the process of becoming; they are not a fixed individual quality (Schonert-Reichl, 2000; Catterall, 1998). Smink & Schargel (2004) prefer to use the term 'at risk' to depict a situation rather than an individual. Periods of transition can both provide the possibility of growth and increase risk situations to be negotiated (Rutter, 1994; Schonert-Reichl, 2000).

The concept of resilience is currently seen by some of as a way out of the problems associated with studying youth risk. One common definition of resilient youth are those who remain competent despite predicted patterns of misfortune and stress (Werner & Smith, 1992). There are many other definitions, which will be discussed later.

Indeed, the study of resilience has the potential to open up the concept of *being* to that which is anomalous (all vulnerable youth do not fail). It also has the possibility to animate *becoming* narratives, which tell us that not all vulnerable young people necessarily remain vulnerable. How do they do this? What is the story? Catterall (1998) suggests that risk be assessed as grounded in actual fluctuating performance rather than be assessed by abstract categories relating to probabilities of failure. In studying grade 8 students over time in the United States, he found that those who were doing poorly in school could turn themselves around by grade 10. To do so, young people require care, support, security, high expectations, school responsiveness, student engagement in school, and opportunities for meaningful participation (Catterall, 1998; Keating & Hertzman, 1999; Werner & Smith, 1992). Thus, tensions between risk and resilience require notation and sorting in youth studies. A further such analysis is offered in Chapter 7.

It is sufficient here to say that resiliency can become a new label 'in lamb's clothing'. What if we see resilient youth rather than resilient situations and contexts? Will we begin to look at what is wrong with young people when they are not resilient? If so, we are back to a simplistic and individual drawing board. One way out is to hold on to the idea of complex cultural nests in studying the transitions young people make (Tilleczek et al., 2010). For example, young people may move from elementary to secondary school while at the same time transitioning from childhood to adulthood and transitioning through their communities and families and into the labour market. As a result, we should examine the wider issues of the ongoing fits or disjunctures between schools, communities, and the lives of children rather than simply targeting student habits and academics as the problematic point. Transitions are not, therefore, a reified problem to be solved; instead, transitions are seen as complicated, as an ongoing tension to be understood and discussed.

In summary, the fundamental social process of *being* is present and useful. Social science has yet to do it justice but should take lessons from the arts and humanities. However, youth studies are generating a good deal of discussion and research relating to self, agency, negotiation, and experience, which demonstrate the importance of *being*. The social process of *becoming* is also needed. We have gained a view to how young people (and those closest to them) are in process. The current work from my research team is illustrating youth's cravings for fresh starts and re-engagements (Tilleczek et al., 2010). How do we build scaffolds and supports for independence and fresh starts? How do we honour and recognize who young people are now without wanting them to simply be more, to get a haircut, to do well in school, to get a job?

By remaining aware of complex cultural nests, we can take a longer conceptual view. Practices such as teaching or guidance could address the complexity and abundance of being. Too often we focus on *being* only for the purposes of directing becoming and not for understanding the true character of the story. *Becoming*, while most often privileged in youth studies, remains as a linear notion that forecloses on process and the complexity of plot. Youth studies could do better to attend seriously and simultaneously to the fundamental social processes of being, becoming, and belonging. How do these processes operate? How do communities of beings in which young people live create or negate the processes of becoming and belonging?

Fountains of Youth: A Composite Youth Testimonial

This section provides examples of the concepts of cultural nests, being, becoming, and belonging based on the findings from the *Early School Leavers Project* (see Tilleczek, 2008d, for more detail). This study examined the lived experiences of 193 young people who left school prior to receiving a diploma, and it invited detailed conversations with young people about their experiences and negotiations through high schools and communities. These youth-driven discussions were about schooling but included the many contexts that intersect with it: in communities and families, with friends, and in the media. The research team invited these young people (aged 16 to 22 years) to begin speaking about their early school leaving from any place they wished. We held at bay our judgments about where this would start or end, and we suspended the view that school leaving was necessarily a problem. We attempted to see their situations in schools as exotic and not 'normal' even though we had read thousands of pages relating to the topic. The young people shared with us their struggles and joys. The youth in this study were from different regions, social classes, cultures, visibility statuses, genders, age groups, and sexual orientations. There was an abundance of *being* in these stories just as there was concurrence of experience.

A brief synopsis of what we learned has been shared in this chapter in the form of 'postcards from high school'. These 'postcards' have been created from a pastiche of stories that formed composite testimonials from the young people (see Tilleczek, 2007a). They are composite narratives in that they represent the collective voices of many young people who shared similar stories, and this common experience has been voiced as one postcard message. The messages are intended to be read in comparison to the other postcards, which represent the composite voices of other groups of young people with different and yet still similar stories to tell. Thus, we hear, on reading across the postcards, the sameness and the variation of the stories told by young people who left school early.

Testimonial narratives are used to bring into focus the importance of what these young people said and the stories they told. We are asked to be witnesses to these stories. It occurred to me that we still look forward to receiving postcards or email messages from our loved ones as they visit exotic destinations. The narrative that is the postcard is well known to us. It succinctly greets us with a brief note to tell of the fun and challenge of a current journey. Combined with a visual image of a recently visited place of interest, it provides an essence of the trip that day. I have therefore used this visual narrative method to assist in suspending our familiarity with high schools and the lives of young people. In treating schools as exotic destinations from which a group of young people eagerly tell about their experiences to loving listeners, this method both informs and jars us.

As mentioned, these young people had similar and dissimilar stories to tell. They all recounted a process of disengagement from school, which led to early school leaving. They all spoke about the process while touching on multiple levels across systems. They all spoke about their interest in education, even if their schools were not necessarily of value to them. Virtually each of the 193 youth wanted to return to education some day, and some had already made concrete plans to do when we spoke. Differences were evident, however, in the ways in which they experienced challenges and positive encounters within and outside the school. Some, for example, disengaged after an illness, sexual assault, overt racism, ongoing classism, troubles at home, school violence, feelings of isolation, academic struggle, or negative relationships with teachers. Some were surrounded by a solid community of beings who worked together to provide needed supports. All of the young people were negotiating their own particular transitions. They told us that a more proactive, flexible, and caring set of cultural nests would have assisted them with their school, home, and community struggles. We will return to the findings of this and other similar studies in Chapter 6.

Dear Principal X:

Please be nice to the teachers. Many of them are my best friends and I like school, I like earning my credits and pulling good marks. It's not that they are not doing their job. It's that they can only do so much. You know? This is a hard business.

Sincerely, Rodney

Dear Mr. Branch: I feel so different here. I need more time to do things and everyone else picks it up right away and I am behind all of the time. I am always behind on everything and I am not even doing easy homework now because I am so overwhelmed by it. . . . You know that I understand and I am smart. I am just overwhelmed, behind, and frustrated. Grrrrrrr. Abdul

Hi Sis, You will love this place. At this school, the teacher takes the topic and relates it to something you like. So, for physics laws, they take what I'm interested in, so my BMX bike becomes a law of physics. They teach you that way and it is fun! They guide you and they also make you feel really important. . . . I can even talk to some of these teachers about the stuff that goes on at home. . . . Who knew that teachers could have such positive impact on my life????

Happy Hugs. . . . Michel XXXOOOOX

Hey, Jorge: You won't believe what I saw today——I saw the most horrible thing today in school. a kid was getting taunted so bad in class that he had to run out of class. he was crying his eyes out and felt awful. He got a death threat too. a note passed to him. It shocked him and shocked us. The teacher should have done something about that but he didn't. He let it happen right in that classroom. I am shaking from this. . . . Joe.

Dear Uncle Stefan: A really funny day today. I got a holiday, an extra vacation, just for skipping class so much. They have kicked me out. I guess that I will never catch up now. But, I got a reward for being such a pain in the ass—they want to get rid of me. The other kids seem angry about this—getting a reward—they should be. . . . I am angry, too, when I really think about it. My education is slipping away and I know I will miss it. . . .

Any suggestions?

Kareem

Hey Pamela: I am coming back to the reserve where everybody gets along. As soon as I left home, I got so many funny looks . . . or certain comments toward Native people and I don't think it's right. It is easier at home and I want to come home and stay with Mom. Can I get my high school diploma from home? I miss you guys a whole lot. . . . Love, Suzette

Dear Mr. R:

I know that you have been teaching kids for a lot of years. You are a good teacher, funny and warm and we really love this class. Could you tell the guidance people that more and more kids these days DO want to become something! I don't mean just lawyers and astronauts and firefighters and all of that. We wanna make a good change for the world. Thanks for helping,

Maeve

Hi Dad: You have to know how I am always so afraid at this school. I have 30 others kids in my class this year and I am always afraid that I will say something wrong. I know that they are all going to laugh at me every time I speak, and I am so-o-o stressed. . . . Paolo

Hey brother Jean-Paul:

Here I am in grade 7 and I finally learned long division. It is just like you said. This is the greatest thing in the world. Wow, this is so cool it's like this machine on paper, and you just like put a number on the top of the machine, and the machine does this trick, and then spits out a number, and there's the answer. I hope we can play with this a bit before it gets turned into worksheets and homework and a bore!

Love ya, K.

Dear Ms. J;

Well, here I am in grade 9, pregnant with my first child. I am only 14 but I feel so old and tired out. I remember thinking that I would have a little doll, would dress her up and show her off so people knew I was loved. That is what the older girls who are 16 or 17 did with their kids. This is so hard to be at school and be with baby K. You were right about all of the real life responsibility that I would have. I hope I make it so she can be proud and be supported and have a good place in the world.

Sincerely, Hoshimi

Dear Mrs. P.:

At home right now, there are a lot of problem with my sister. She is putting a lot of stress on my father and he is starting to get sick. I have to leave school to take care of him. I know that my mom could not take care of me when I was little so I need to learn to take care of other people. I guess I will not be able to finish my homework or go on the class trip. I wish that I could.

Thanks for your help. I need it. . . . Karolina

Dear Auntie: I do not like the school in this country. Some of the children and teachers are nice. But others are very mean and unhelpful. Mother and Father cannot help me with English and I am much behind where I was in school at home. Today the teacher was helping us with a problem on the blackboard and I began to explain it. The whole class started laughing at me because of the way I speak English. I need support at home and at school. But how can I get it? Do you have advice for me?

Love, Ponthioun

Hi Mom: You need to know that there is racism at school too. Today the principal expelled 2 more Hispanic and Black students in the school. The majority of them seem to be expelled. He is telling them to leave the school. School is a place where they watch too close and care too little. There are like 45 cameras in the school . . . we have a little police station there too . . . probably because there was a lot of black people there. I don't know. . . . Does it get any better out there? I thought we were fighting racism? Love Justin

Dear Aishah: Things are no better. Today a Black kid who was wearing a chain (like a rapper heavy duty neck chain) was told by the principal that he had to take it off, because anyone who wore those kinds of chains was in a gang. . . . Then, she suspended him for two weeks. . . . He mostly got those two weeks because he argued to the fact that . . . his friends, who indeed where uh, White . . . were wearing them and she hadn't bothered them at all. Talking back was right, but not for him. It is unreal.

Talk soon, Chung

Hi Mom:

I feel so down. It's very, very easy for me to become depressed, and I stop liking myself, liking who I am . . . it is spreading to other areas of my life . . . I need the help at home and school to address these issues at the beginning before they balloon. And it's so difficult to do because so many of the symptoms or whatnot are invisible—it is a mental illness and I need help.

Love, Susan

Mrs G: Help!
Now I am taking the responsibility for caring for younger siblings because they are getting neglected. Then, my stepfather was very, like, a drunk and he almost stabbed me with a knife because he's so bad. . . . You know how much I enjoy school. I want to go to school. I'm stuck in a hole where it's hard to go to school and survive 'cause out here I need to learn to have a job, still do homework, take care of all of these people. . . . What can I do???????? Trevor

Critical Thinking Activities

1. Write the word *child* on one side of a page of paper and draw an arrow connecting it to the word *adult* on the far side of the same page. Now, think of the ways you have moved from one to the other in your life. What

rites of passage have you moved through? What people, places, and things influenced you? What did you experience? What actions have you taken to negotiate your own transitions? Did you experience complex cultural nests in your life? Explain. Once you have completed this exercise, save your work in a place it can be easily found. You will be asked to return to it at the end of the book.

2. Which paintings and images can you find that directly illustrate the tensions of *being*, *becoming*, and *belonging*? Explain how these images do so. Find three additional images that illustrate these tensions.

3. What is the complex cultural nesting approach, and how could it assist in understanding youth studies in a contemporary context? Use the postcard narratives as examples of your understanding or critique of the approach.

4. Attempt to make sense of the postcards provided in this chapter for the complex cultural nesting approach. What do they seem to suggest about the experiences and structures that young people encounter at school, at home, and in the community?

Further Readings

Bronfenbrenner, U. (Ed.) (2005). *Making Human Beings Human: Bioecological Perspectives on Human Development*. Thousand Oaks, CA: Sage Publications.

Cohen & Ainley. (2000). In the country of the blind: Youth studies and cultural studies in Britain. In J. Pickford (Ed.). *Youth Justice: Theory and Practice*. London: Cavendish Publishing Ltd.

Griffin, C. (1993). *Representations of Youth: The Study of Youth and Adolescence in Britain and America*. Oxford: Polity Press.

Tilleczek, K., Ferguson, B., Rummens, J.A., & Boydell, K. (2006). How do youth leave school? Current lessons from youth who know. *Education Canada*, 54–57.

Suggested Websites

Canadian Council on Learning
www.ccl-cca.ca/CCL/Home/index.htm?Language=EN

Images of Urie Bronfenbrenner's Ecological Systems Theory
http://pt3.nl.edu/paquetteryanwebquest.pdf

Chapter Two

Historical and Mythic Foundations for Youth Studies

I see no hope for the future of our people if they are dependent on frivolous youth of today, for certainly all youth are reckless beyond words... When I was young, we were taught to be discreet and respectful of elders, but the present youth are exceedingly wise [disrespectful] and impatient of restraint. (Hesiod, eighth century BCE)

In this book we have described a number of changes that have occurred that helped obscure the essential continuities in the structure of social life and which often mask the processes of social reproduction. These changes have promoted individual responsibilities and weakened collectivist traditions and made the language of social class appear antiquated. (Furlong & Cartmel, 2007: 139)

Introduction

This chapter of the book acquaints readers with the foundations, myths, and history of youth studies. The aim is to explore youth studies and the socio-historic influences that impinge upon youth and with which youth interact and actively negotiate. The concept of culture is more fully examined. The crux of this section is to explore the different ways in which society's ideas about youth influence how we treat our young. The chapter will outline bi-directional concepts that show how young people act in relation to these societal functions. For instance, we now live in a culture where 'being young' is paradoxical: while a majority of adults wish to remain forever young, we do not necessarily treat actual young people with respect. Many adults want to preserve the biological aspects of youth (that is, with plastic surgery to look young); they seek lifestyles of freedom from responsibility at the same time that they hold the balance of power in society. Moreover, adults have often chastised youth for being irresponsible and 'young' while they co-opt the posture for themselves. I agree with Cohen (1999), who sees the lines between childhood and adulthood becoming increasingly blurred.

This chapter therefore explores three of the foundational myths that suggest how we have landed here. It then goes on to provide a brief social history of youth and youth studies as a context for the debates and content to come. The final section provides a summary of foundational ideas from Chapters 1 and 2, which are presented as a set of propositions for discussion.

Follies and Myths

Neglecting the complexity and abundance of youth is not the only problem that youth studies has had, but it is a particularly burdensome one, as is evident in the myriad ways its study is absent in the field. Lee (1998) has wisely suggested a move toward embracing an 'immature' social science that allows for the recognition of the *unfinished* and *incomplete* aspects of people and contexts. For example, he suggests a more pointed examination of those aspects of the social world that are becoming or coming into being. Moreover, disciplines such as sociology, history, and psychology have been shown to have privileged the study of adults over that of young people, who are marginalized by comparison. Whereas social inequalities have been examined and commented upon by many scholars, age has taken a back seat to serious study, as have the intersections of social class, gender, and ethnicity in studying youth.

There are three identifiable and related fallacies and myths in youth studies: (1) the epistemological fallacy of modern society; (2) the myth that being a youth is necessarily risky, stormy, and stressful; and (3) the myth that our current notions of youth have always been with us. Each myth is introduced here and will be further detailed in the book with an eye to recognizing the follies and fallacies of youth studies.

The Epistemological Fallacy of Modern Society

The first fallacy has been well documented by Furlong and Cartmel (2007), who have coined the term 'epistemological fallacy' as it relates to youth studies. Their work demonstrates this concept by showing how we have come to hide the important cultural relations that impinge on young people and instead foreground individual and subjective levels of analyses:

> Our central thesis is that while traditional sources of inequality continue to ensure the reproduction of advantage and disadvantage for the younger generation, various social changes have meant that these social cleavages have become obscure. Moreover, young people increasingly

perceive themselves as living in a society characterized by risk and uncertainty which they expect to have to negotiate on an individual level. (p. 12)

Cohen and Ainley (2000) agrees and shows that one such social change is the field of youth studies itself. He shows how youth studies has taken a happy but troubling step toward individualistic analysis in the past decade. He traces these changes to the post-modern theoretical movements in cultural studies and the group of scholars who began to focus solely on youth as a discourse rather than as a set of complex social actions. The negative outcome has been in overlooking how inequality is reproduced for young people in modern society. But Beck (1992) suggests there are many contradictions that need to be attended to, such as the expansion in wealth alongside the growing incidence of health problems, especially for those marginalized by social class and age. Keating and Hertzman (1999) have detailed this issue in Canada and globally as 'modernity's paradox' and provide a wealth of data showing that developmental health of young people remains tied to their social class and material conditions. Many youth remain in potentially vulnerable positions, and ceasing our analysis in the discourse does little to understand emerging or ongoing modern vulnerabilities.

The accumulation of evidence for this argument will be explored in later chapters. For now, I note that focus on the macrosystem and chronosystem have shown that modernity is characterized by a weakening of social networks that traditionally supported young people (Beck, 1992). Transitions to adulthood are therefore increasingly multidimensional, nonlinear, and complicated (Furlong & Cartmel, 2007; Tilleczek & Lewko, 2001). However, lifestyles have become individualized and problems perceived as outcomes of individual failings solved only through individual rather than collective action. Thus, Furlong and Cartmel (2007) show that an important feature of modern society is a fallacy of individual control that hides the social relations between people and the institutions that govern them. It is critical to examine these social relations in unique ways (Cohen, 1999; Kinsman, 2006; Smith, 2002) and place the everyday experiences of young people at the nexus of research. This will be the focus of Chapter 4.

Being a Youth Is Necessarily Risky, Stormy, and Stressful

The second myth is that the youth period is necessarily stormy, stressful, and risky. These ideas have long a long history, which began with the work of G.S. Hall in 1904. As the following section and Chapter 7 will detail, the social history of youth and youth studies provides a window onto the origins and fallout of this myth. Indeed, most current texts about young people and adolescence cite Hall, the American psychologist, as the founder of the scholarly study of youth and adolescence by pointing to his influential two-volume set, *Adolescence: Its Psychology and Its Relation to Physiology, Anthropology and Sociology, Sex, Crime, Religion, and Education*. While stunning in its reach and ambition, Arnett (2010) points out that scholars, such as Youniss (2006), see the work as largely outdated. Others (cf. Côté & Allahar, 2006; and Tyyska, 2009) show how the work is outdated in terms of its theoretical direction in insisting on recapitulation and the negative or problematic dimensions of youth. Of course, we are able to see in the social historical records the examination of youth in ancient Greece by Plato and Aristotle and therefore wonder if 1904 marked the beginning of the serious scholarly study of youth. In addition, the important and ongoing work of anthropologists has demonstrated the roles that culture plays in setting up and interpreting social situations for youth. Margaret Mead's critical anthropological work in Samoa in the 1920s raised serious issue with G.S. Hall's interpretation about youth and suggested that youth were not necessarily or fundamentally stormy and stressful beings. In the following passages, Mead summarizes her 1928 work, *Coming of Age in Samoa:*

> With a background of knowledge about Samoan custom, of the way in which a child is educated, of the claims which the community makes upon children and young people, of the attitude towards sex and personality, we come to the tale of the group of girls with whom I spent many months, the group of girls between ten and 20 years of age who lived in the three little villages on the lee side of the island of Tau. In their lives as a group, in their responses as individuals, lays the answer to the question: What is coming of age like in Samoa?
>
> All of these children had seen birth and death. They had all seen many dead bodies. They had watched miscarriages and peeked under the arms of the old women who were washing and commenting on the underdeveloped foetus.
>
> In matters of sex the ten-year-olds are equally sophisticated, although they witness sex activities only surreptitiously, since all expressions of affections are barred in public. But the lack of privacy within the houses where mosquito netting marks off purely formal walls about married couples, and the custom of young couples using the palm grove for their rendezvous, makes it inevitable that children should see intercourse, often and between many people . . .
>
> With the exception of a few cases . . . adolescence represented no period of crisis or stress, but was instead an orderly developing set of slowly maturing interests and activities. The girls' minds were perplexed by no conflicts, troubled by no philosophical queries, beset by no remote ambitions. To live as a girl with as many lovers as long as possible and then to marry in one's own village near one's own relatives and to have many children, these were uniform and satisfying ambitions. *(pp. 131–135, p. 157)*

That Our Current Concept of Youth Has Always Been with Us

The third myth is that the concept of youth has been with us throughout history. The historical analysis to debunk this myth is the main focus of the following section. Suffice it to say here that while some things have remained the same, there are many differences in understandings, conceptualizations, and treatments of young people across history. Attending to historical contexts, similarities, and differences allows for a more thorough understanding of youth studies in a contemporary context.

A Brief Social History

Youth is an idea that has been both continuous and discontinuous over the ages. Many comprehensive social histories have been written about youth, and in 2008 the *Journal of the History of Childhood and Youth* was launched to publish original scholarly work in the field. In 2007, moreover, the British Broadcasting Corporation (BBC) also launched a far-reaching website relating to its ongoing discussions of the history of childhood and youth. However, few works have attempted critical social histories of youth in Canada. (Among the more interesting are Comacchio, 2006, and Sutherland, Barmond & Hale, 1992.) Phillip Ariès's groundbreaking work, *Centuries of Childhood*, began to show how variably youth has been represented across social history (Ariès, 1962). Many social historians begin with his work and add critique and substance to the field.

A complete review of all youth histories is not the purpose here. Rather, the selection and synthesis of works is presented to exemplify the similarities, differences, continuities, and discontinuities in the treatment and understanding of youth over time. Of particular importance are the four social events arising from political, economic, and social transformations uncovered in this work and seen to most profoundly influence young people today: compulsory education; the youth justice movement; the children's rights movement; and the proliferation of digital and global influences. Moreover, the way in which youth are imagined to be and act is uncovered. The dance between reason and passion, the tensions in being and becoming, and the debates about the good and evil of youth permeate the social historical work.

Arentt (2010) maps out a brief but useful overview of the history of youth as understood in ancient Greece. Both Plato and Aristotle left records of their thoughts about the period of youth (ages 14–21) as a time when reason first develops in earnest and instincts are therefore potentially overcome. In Book II of *Rhetoric*, Aristotle provides a detailed description of the character of youth as a dance between wisdom and passion, which can be examined in comparison to the experiences and ideas of youth today:

Young men are of such a character as to have strong desires and as such they tend to satisfy their desires. Of the bodily desires, they pursue sex most of all and are incontinent about it. They are changeable and fickly in their desires, which are strong but end quickly. Their wishes are intense but shallow, like those of sick people who are thirsty or hungry. They are quick-tempered and hot-tempered and tend to give vent to their temper; and their temper gets the better of them, for because of their love of honour, they cannot bear being belittled but are indignant if they think they are unjustly treated. They love honour, but they love victory even more; for youth desires superiority over others and victory is a form of superiority . . . They are not malicious but well-meaning because they have not witnessed many instances of wickedness. They tend to trust others because they have not often been deceived. They are hopeful; for, like intoxicated persons, they are warm blooded by nature and also because they have not yet failed often. Their life is filled with expectation, expectation is of future things whereas memory is things past, and youth has a long future before it but a short past behind it . . . they love too much, they hate too much and likewise with all other things. And they think they know everything and are quite sure about it; and indeed this is the reason for overdoing everything. And they act unjustly for the sake of insult and not for the sake of harm. And they are disposed to pity others because they regard them as kind or better; . . . for they measure their neighbors by their own unwillingness to harm others and hence regard them as not deserving to suffer. And they are fond of laughing and so are witty; for wit is a cultivated insult. Such, then, is the character of youth. (Aristotle, 1987: 1389a-b)

Hendrick (2001) has provided a social history to explore some of the origins of these notions emerging from the 1600s. He places the neo-Platonist philosophers' assertions about the innate goodness of the child at the centre of a movement toward Locke's 1693 *Some Thoughts Concerning Education*, in which children were not all the same and were open to ideas, education, and guidance. In Rousseau's 1762 *Emile,* a new affection and understanding was bestowed upon young people. The insistence on the nature and singularity of an understanding of the child for the child's own sake was to be seen as critical in education and parenting. However, Hendrick (2001) also shows how the importance of understanding the child as *being* was lost in the practice of some reformers, whose interpretation of *Emile* was to see young people as naturally incapable and vulnerable. In meeting up with the Romantics in the late 1700s, this idea of 'original innocence' unfolded more stridently in the search for understanding the sources of youthful innocence (for example, the works of Blake) or the essence of virtue and innocence in the child (for example, the works of Wordsworth). As Hendrick states these notions went underground during the 1800's:

Poets are no match for political economy. Both the reaction of the French Revolution—the suppression of liberties—and the impact of the industrial revolution—the demand for free labour and the destruction of the old 'moral economy'—pushed child-adult relations in the opposite direction to that promised by the Romantic aspiration. Besides the reactionary political climate of the early nineteenth century and the aggressiveness of the new capitalism, optimistic notions of childhood also found themselves pitted against the weight of Evangelical Revival, with its belief in Original Sin and the need for redemption. In evangelical hands, human nature, having been tarnished from the fall from grace, was no longer 'pleasing to the author of Being'. Thus, the 1799 *Evangelical Magazine* taught parents to teach their children that they 'are sinful polluted creatures'. (p. 38)

Moving into contemporary contexts and relating more directly to youth studies today, we recognize the continuation of these fissures and debates. As stated earlier, the work of G.S. Hall in the United Sates at the beginning of the twentieth century (1904) is normally the demarcation in North America of the 'invention of adolescence'. A host of scholars begin their historical sketches with this work and make the point that it is essentially a conception of behaviour imposed upon youth rather than an empirical assessment of the ways in which young people behaved (Comacchio, 2006; Côté & Allahar, 2006; Demos & Demos, 1969; Gillis, 1981; Kett, 1977; Sebald, 1992). For example, it has been stated that 'the architects of adolescence used biology and psychology (specifically Hall's metaphor of "storm and stress") to justify the promotion of young people to norms of behaviour that were freighted with middle-class values' (Kett, 1977: 243).

The unwanted conduct of youth in Hall's day was assessed according to three related norms: conformity, anti-intellectuality, and passivity. This is especially noteworthy since Hall's theoretical work spilled out 'past the university walls' (Enright, 1987: 554) to influence movements such as the Boy Scouts and the YMCA. As we will see in Comacchio's (2006) work, Hall's work also influenced practices and treatments of young people in Canada. In the period from 1900 to 1920 in North America, the 'collective coercion of bodies' approach as described by Foucault (1977) came to be a solution to the problematic and troubled nature of youth. Boys were thought to be 'growing wild and slightly criminal' and secondary schools were encouraged to correct their behaviour by providing 'rifle practice and military maneuvers' (Hall, 1918: 306, cited in Enright et al., 1987). The historical evidence illustrates that childlike passivity was enforced for youth during times of depression; and adultlike activity, during times of war. Two useful examples illustrate this critical historical approach.

One of the more useful examples is the work of Enright, Levy, Harris, and Lapsley (1987) who explored links between theory generation, history, and societal images of youth. In reviewing close to 100 academic articles written about youth encompassing two economic depressions and two world wars, their data indicate the following relationship:

> In times of economic depression, theories of adolescence emerge that portray teenagers as immature, psychologically unstable, and in need of prolonged participation in the educational system. During wartime, the psychological competence of youth is emphasized and the duration of education is recommended to be more retracted than in depression. (p. 541)

During World Wars I and II, adolescence was seen as an adultlike stage that develops quickly and should be accelerated. In times of war, this idea of adolescence is not difficult to understand. Indeed, it would have been much more troubling to publicly send children to the front lines of the war; youth were conveniently regarded as young adults. However, during the depressions of the 1890s and 1930s, youth emerged as a phase that was both stressful and childlike. Since work was too scarce for adult males, youth were caught up in a back-to-school movement. Keeping them within the confines of the education system was one way to protect the work of adults. These images then reversed under economic fluctuation and demand for a growing labour force. For a modern example, one needs only to pay attention to Alberta's pushing and pulling of the youth labour force via fluctuating working age and minimum wage to attract/repel young people into/out of the labour market during that province's economic boom/bust.

Another example of a social history of youth comes more recently from a Canadian context. In fact, Comacchio (2006) offers the first detailed study of youth in early-twentieth-century Canada. Her work demonstrates how young Canadians of this time were seen as the nation's first fully *modern* teenagers. Like Enright et al., she suggests that Canadian youth debates and treatments took form from 1920 to 1950 because in 'each of the three decades . . . a world crisis—the Great War, the Great Depression, [and] World War II—proved the necessary trigger for . . . a generational consciousness' (p. 8). Anuik's 2008 review of the book points out that the work well demontrates the emergence of a moral paradox in that youth were 'expected to grow into strong and morally-upright citizens but had to compromise their development with the adults who believed they were responsible for their development' (Anuik, 2008: 301–03). Adults deployed citizenship as a means to control and to redirect what were still seen to be 'problematic youth', suggesting that most theorists at this time considered adolescence to be 'a problem of alarming scope and potential' (Comacchio, 2006: 21). Comacchio situates citizenship as a metaphor for a 'young Canada', a nation that could be considered an adolescent still 'figuring itself out'. She provides historical evidence to suggest that by the end of the 1930s, the professionals who studied youth across the world synthesized their thoughts into a 'nature and nurture' paradigm. She suggests that this led to the proliferation and application of terms such as *delinquent* and *deviant* to what were perceived to be problematic youth (members of racial minorities, immigrants, and those of non-middle-class and non-Christian backgrounds). Schissel's (2007) contemporary work on the youth justice system and the media's representations of youth in Saskatchewan show that this is still too often the case. Schissel describes the moral panics that continue to surround the 'young folk devils' of today wherein young people take on the characteristics of demons and are painted with the same brush as being restless, reckless, and dangerous to society.

Similar to the treatment of at-risk youth today, the young Canadians in the early part of 1900s were subject to individualized interventions (Commachio, 2006). For example, Comacchio maps out the Canadian process of longer-term stays at home and more time spent in school, two structural changes that continue into contemporary contexts (Furlong & Cartmel, 2007). Today, a whole host of concepts such as 'emerging adulthood' (cf. Arnett, 2010) are being employed to illustrate the prolonged youth and social holding tanks of young people. The proliferation of young people as NEETS (Not in Employment, Education, or Training) in the United Kingdom demonstrates that more and more youth are becoming marginalized in modern society. Like Enright et al. (1987), Comacchio shows that these extensions to the coming-of-age process became most visible during the Depression years when large numbers of students, who would have departed formal education after the completion of grade eight, remained in class in order to avoid entering a desolate labour market. Compulsory education was therefore elongated and, as Anuik (2008) has noted, used to invoke in young people the ideal of citizenship by teaching topics such as sex, work and loyalty to the war effort.

The shift from youth as political 'problems' that need to be contained to youth as nothing but consumers has been illustrated in many analyses. Comacchio focuses on the rise of the contemporary youth as consumer in the 1920s, the first era when the private sector recognized youth's purchasing power. This consumer culture of youth has continued into the present day with global capital expansion. Profit takes primacy over the needs and rights of the environment, of the land, and of young people (McNally, 2002), which has led to the pervasive culture of commodification and consumption. Especially for youth who have access to media technology and disposable income, lives are gated into low-paying 'McJobs' and mass consumption of the latest US invention. Youth culture has become synonymous with purchasing ever-changing fashion, music, and technologies (Latham 2002). Television advertisements and films no longer attempt to hide the agenda even as evidence shows that the more youth engage in consumer culture, the greater may be their feelings of helplessness (Schor, 2004).

Another notable trend of the early 1900s in Canada was the rise of the 'club movement', such as the Christian-influenced Girl Guides and Boy Scouts. Secular social spaces also began to be designed for 'safe' contact between young people. These clubs represented 'the normalization and institutionalization of the distinctive life stage that was modern adolescence' (Comacchio, 2006: 208) and were firmly in place by the end of World War II. Similar reverberations are felt today with the highly organized and institutionalized forms of leisure offered to youth (Furlong & Cartmel, 2007), a movement meant to continue to provide safe and sanctioned activity.

These tensions, between active growth and passive conformity and between continuity and discontinuity, continue. Current dominant representations of youth set them apart from children and adults, suggest homogeneity of experience, the inevitability of trouble, and the constant need for surveillance (Griffen, 1997; Kelly, 2000). For example, sex education curricula knots danger and pleasure together through unclear messages that simultaneously normalize and pathologize intimate encounters (Alexander, 2007; Marecek, 2002). Such mixed messages wield embodied contradictions of young people as active/passive, good/bad, and capable/incapable. In reading much of the current adolescent development literature of the past 50 years, one has the impression that Margaret Mead's pioneering work in Samoa has too often been neglected.

This lack of attention to cultural influences continues to limit youth studies. Often cited in contemporary psychological discussions are the 'risk-taking' propensity of youth and 'faulty adolescent cognition'. The literature portrays youth as necessarily a time of escalating and troubling risk-taking (Irwin, 1993; Muuss & Porton, 1998). The wealth of research aimed at explaining the causes of risk-taking behaviour include a general cognitive incapability (unrealistic self-appraisal and cognitive egocentrism), the inability to perceive risks, thrill-seeking personality variables, and family structure (Arnett & Balle-Jensen, 1993). However, as is detailed in Chapter 7, this is not the whole story and is a faulty one at best. Risk is not necessarily problematic but plays an important part in the positive growth and development of young people. In fact, young people use risk as cultural 'edgework', allowing negotiations between self and others (Lyng, 1993). Risk is both social and transformative, taking the place of childhood play for social growth (Lightfoot, 1997). Contemporary models arising from the social history of youth as incompetent deviants require further scrutiny.

Summary: Ten Reflections on Youth Studies

Part One of this book has provided foundations, follies, and social historical contexts for youth studies. In so doing, the myths about young people have been presented along with a suggested approach—complex cultural nesting—that may help to organize and enact a critical consideration for youth studies.

The central ideas of *being, becoming,* and *belonging* have also been introduced to keep clear the tensions, problems, and issues as they occur when working *with* and *for* young people. The central ideas of the first chapters of the book are presented below. They form a summary and a set of reflective propositions for debate and discussion.

1. Young people and the study of youth have varied across cultural and historical contexts. There are both continuities and discontinuities. Biological immaturity and growth is universal and continuous, but the meanings, models, and methods of youth study are not necessarily so, nor are the ways that young people are treated or act.

2. There is real value in rigorous study of young people. The ways in which they are actively negotiating their social lives—and not just how adults have constructed life for them—are critical to the study of youth. This aspect of youth studies is often ignored.

3. Complex cultural nests hold the experiences, structures, and timing of continuities and discontinuities of youth. Youth studies cannot be separated from the lived experiences of the social organization and reproduction of ethnicity, social class, age, race, region, sexualities, or gender and their intersections.

4. Complex cultural nests take into consideration the intersections of social class, age, race, region, ethnicity, sexuality, and gender at multiple levels of systems while focusing on the micro-level experiences of young people at the meso level. The meso level is the liminal zone where we can best observe the embodiment, interaction, and coming together of systems (chrono, macro, and micro).

5. The epistemological fallacy of modern society tends to obscure such analyses by attending to individual issues and problems that are in fact organized in social, political, economic, and cultural structures.

6. *Being* is a useful concept in that it reminds us to observe and value the everyday life experiences of young people. Young people can be taken at their word, examined and valued for who they are *now*. It is also critical to examine identity processes and individualization at the heart of *being*. Communities of beings surround young people at each level and create or negate the belonging that is critical to them.

7. *Becoming* is also a useful concept in that it reminds us that young people and youth studies are also shifting and are in flux across time (however they wish to define it). These shifts can be conceptualized as nested transitions. Flexible, complex, nuanced trajectories and pathways are the channels by which we witness *becoming*.

8. Transitions have often been mistakenly conceptualized to be simple, linear, and leading to a specific kind of 'successful end point' as defined

by the state, by government officials, by parents, or by educators. Young people should instead be asked to articulate their own goals and dreams. Transitions are nested, complex, and nonlinear, which can be seen in the stories and biographies of youth as they intersect with the cultures and structures they negotiate. Transitional points in the lives of young people are important locations of study, and their meanings and processes require further elaboration.

9. The main preoccupations of youth studies are culture, development, and praxis.

10. Research and practice are often separated and targeted at only one or another level without seeing the interconnections, cultural nests, or nested transitions young people negotiate. Methods and practices that allow us to find a way forward to praxis for youth studies and a way to enact practices *with* and *for* young people are the focus of the next section of the book.

Critical Thinking Activities

1. A valuable way of learning about reflecting on the context and history of youth is to study artistic representations of youth over time. For this activity, conduct an Internet search to find representations of youth from at least three different time periods. For each image, reflect on what it conveys about youth and youth studies in the designated time period.

2. What are the four most important social events in history that help to define the lives of youth today? What are the most important similarities/dissimilarities between today and the past?

3. Write a brief biographical narrative of your own youth and attempt to assess it using the complex cultural nesting approach.

Further Readings

Ariès, P. (1962). *Centuries of Childhood: A Social History of Family Life*. New York: Vintage Books.

Comacchio, C. (2006). *The Dominion of Youth: Adolescence and the Making of a Modern Canada, 1920 to 1950*. Waterloo, ON: Wilfred Laurier University Press.

Hendrick, H. (2001). Constructions and reconstructions of British childhood: An interpretive survey, 1800 to the present. In A. Prout & A. James (Eds), *Constructing and Reconstructing Childhood* (pp. 34–62). London: RoutledgeFalmer.

Mead, M. (1928). *Coming of Age in Samoa*. New York: W. Morrow and Company.

Suggested Websites

BBC: The Invention of Childhood
www.bbc.co.uk/radio4/history/childhood/

Margaret Mead: Samoa: The Adolescent Girl
www.loc.gov/exhibits/mead/field-samoa.html

Part Two

Research with and for Youth: Redressing Praxis, Method, and Theory

Part Two directs attention to important ways in which to understand and study young people and their daily lives in social contexts. Few books about youth studies take up the task of reflecting on how and why we know what we know about young people. Where does our data come from? How can we enter into the process of doing research with and for young people? Where do we start and finish? Research strategies are processes of inquiry and rules of thumb rather than strict and stringent marching orders, and the processes are artistic and creative ones. This section of the book discusses some of the most innovative and critical strategies being used to work with and for young people. In so doing, the relationship between theories and ways of doing research is addressed.

Chapter 3 asks for consideration of how we ask our research questions in the first place, how we answer those questions, and what the answers mean. The chapter provides examples and critiques of theories and methods in youth studies and demonstrates 'praxis' as a coming together of theory and method. The chapter then provides guidelines for three interesting critical social methods for answering research questions (institutional ethnography, critical discourse analysis, and participatory action research). Chapter 4 then follows this opening and examines a possibility for a social science *with* and *for* young people. What does this look like? How do we accomplish this and to what end? What are the means by which we do this work? To address these challenges, Chapter 4 first examines some broad trends in the well-being of contemporary youth in families, work places, communities, and schools, and looks at some of the main stumbling points for youth by intersections of age, socio-economic status, ethnicity, and regional and cultural inequalities. It is suggested that these are the areas that are in need of further critical study, and two examples are provided. Part Two closes with six summary statements for imagining a social science *with* and *for* young people.

Chapter Three

Asking and Answering Good Questions: The Praxis of Youth Studies

Introduction

No text that incorporates analysis and discourse on research, data, and theory is complete without some discussion of social science research methods. This chapter is not intended to provide an exhaustive explanation and discussion of the intricacies of social research methods. It does not replace a formal study of social research methodology but rather begins with a broad brush-stroke treatment of some important definitions to facilitate an understanding of how different research outcomes about young people are arrived at through the application of different methodologies. The Chapter examines some of the origins and assumptions embedded in these methodologies and methods.

Posing Questions *with* and *for* Young People

One of the most difficult aspects of doing social research is asking a 'good' question, knowing how to go about answering it, and understanding what the answers mean. This requires asking and answering a question that is actually 'askable'. That is, the question must relate to an appropriate, well-conceived, and iterative process for answering it. To simplify matters, social research processes can be thought of as those that follow either a qualitative or a quantitative approach. Figure 3.1 illustrates and simplifies these distinctions in social research methods. The examples provided are not exhaustive but leave impressions that quantitative methods are related to the detailed use of numbers and statistics while qualitative methods are related to in-depth discussions, observations, and interpretation of texts via words and images.

But before any such methods are selected and employed there are concepts

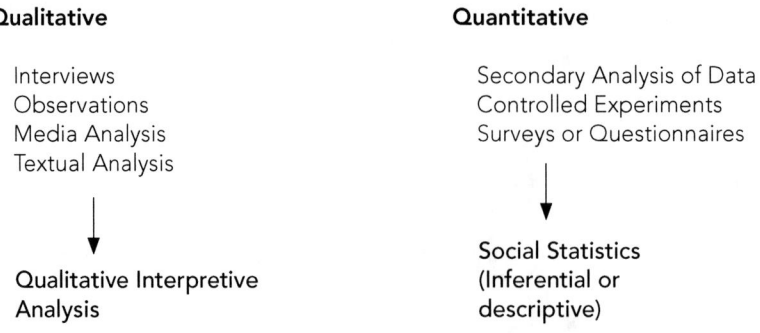

Figure 3.1 Two Strands of Social Research Methods

behind each strand which must be considered. For instance, it is useful to consider

> ethics (axiology), epistemology, ontology, and methodology. Ethics asks, How will I be a moral person in the world? Epistemology asks, How do I know the world? What is the relationship between the inquirer and the known? Every epistemology . . . implies an ethical-moral stance toward the world and the self of the researcher. Ontology raises basic questions about the nature of reality and the nature of the human being in the world. Methodology focuses on the best means for gaining knowledge about the world. (Lincoln & Guba, 2000: 157)

For example, doing in-depth research with young people to understand how school cultures influence their educational achievements could be accomplished via a critical ethnography, which is a methodology that will be discussed later in detail. For now, it is important to know that this is a way to do research where you take up the perspective of those who are marginalized in society and provide a space for them to speak and provide their experiences and stories so that you may see how they are organized socially. Once chosen, critical ethnography's assumptions and methods would be adhered to, such as using a range of qualitative methods (observations, interviews, narrative techniques, art-based creations, etc.). Methods such as narrative interview techniques in conjunction with textual analysis and observation may also be used. The tool kit of methods is selected based on approach or methodology. The selection of approach and methodology is based on other assumptions, the kinds of questions you are asking, and the purpose you have for asking/answering them. Methodology is 'the theory of how inquiry should proceed' (Schwandt, 2007: 193). The assumptions based therein and most often discussed in social research are those relating to **epistemology, ontology,** and **axiology**.

Epistemology is the theory of knowledge or how we come to know what

Interpretive	Positivist
What exists is not always tangible	What exists is absolute and true
Need to interpret the world	Search for causes and regularities
Subjective experience is important	Objective knowledge is important
Methods of interpretation, story, narrative, discussion, art	Methods of probabillity, mathematics, science
Methods should differ from natural science	Methods from natural science
Try to Describe	Try to Predict

Figure 3.2 Two Examples of Epistemology

we know. Figure 3.2 provides a simplistic look at just two examples of epistemology and neither is exhaustive of all that each entails. There are others, such as Indigenous ways of knowing, social constructionism, philosophical hermeneutics, postpositivism, and so forth. Each relates to assumptions about questions such as the following: What can we ask? Why are we asking it? For whom are we doing the research? What is the process by which we can answer our questions? One interesting historical cleavage in discussions of epistemology is whether or not we should use the same methods to study the natural world (the scientific methods of physics, biology, mathematics, etc.) that we use to study the social world (cultures, human experiences, human relations, social contexts, etc.).

Ontology is a connected and important concept in the discussion of social research methods. In that context, the term has to do with a theory of how the social world comes into being. This idea comes from a branch of philosophy known as metaphysics, which is how we understand the nature of reality, a theory of 'being', and the real nature of 'what is' (Schwandt, 2007: 190). In association with the discussion about *being* and *becoming* in youth studies, this concept is worth further examination. For instance, working from a positivist epistemology suggests ontological positions relating to metaphysical 'realism' such that the 'objectivity of science is to know things as they are' (Schwandt, 2007: 210). However, the interpretive theory of knowledge relates more closely to understanding '*Dasein*, or the human being in the social world' (Schwandt, 2007: 190) and could consist of phenomenological positions concerning the understanding of human experience. There are many philosophical understandings of *being* and the concept is much discussed and debated. It has been argued that contemporary social science is marked by a 'return of the metaphysical . . . , a renewed concern with the nature, constitution and structure of being and social reality and how knowledge of same plays a role in our claims to social reality' (Schwandt, 2007: 190).

Perhaps not so straightforward, epistemological and ontological assumptions are nevertheless important in social research. Karl Popper, a philosopher of science, is quoted by his student Paul Feyerabend as saying, 'I am a professor of scientific method—but I have a problem: there is no scientific method. There are some simple rules of thumb, and they are quite helpful' (Feyerabend, 1995: 88). After studying with Popper, Feyerabend went on to write *Against Method* in 1975. Here he continues to speak about how science, once thought to be based on true facts, is itself open to 'anarchy' and often proceeds counterintuitively. He further contends that in a democratic society, 'science should be taught as one view among many and not as the one and only road to truth and reality' (2002: viii). In *Conquest of Abundance: A Tale of Abstraction versus the Richness of Being* (1999) Feyerabend takes this idea further and elegantly illustrates how some methods and their underlying political assumptions have eradicated the abundance, nuance, and complexity that is human existence.

The idea that scientific method is not stringent or trustworthy may not be new to many readers. If science itself is debating method and causality and social science is now distinct from science, where does this leave social research methods? Do we have such methods? Are they precise? How do we make sense of what we learn in our work? Given the above arguments and philosophical discussions about social science, researchers find ways of proceeding to answer their questions and invoking their 'rules of thumb'.

Regardless of the type of approach you take or the rules of thumb you follow, research processes are also preoccupied with praxis and an eye to axiology. The emerging field of youth studies takes a praxis-related approach in which theory, method, and practice are closely linked and thus invoke the mutual creation and use of knowledge about young people. *Praxis* was defined in Chapter 1 and can be found in the book's glossary. Here, *praxis* is further described as relating to the work of critical social inquiry. Practice can take the shape of many things, including political action, teaching, conducting research, writing policy, working in a correctional facility, enabling youth, taking social justice action, advocating, or nursing someone to health. Axiology is about the ethics, value, and political position taken when working in these fields. It arises from the fact–value distinction in philosophy and social science in the debate about whether it is possible to take a 'value-free' location in our work. The politics of research and practice relate to the values and locations of the researcher and what you and others do with your research when it is finished.

While discussions of epistemology, ontology, and axiology can appear cumbersome at times, they are critical pieces of the process of youth studies in contemporary contexts. One important idea is that the practice of research and its applications link theories and assumptions to methods and processes to applications and further practice. This is the praxis of youth studies that may be accomplished for the understanding, explaining, hearing, and advancement of young people.

> ## Box 3.1 Writing Research Questions in Youth Studies
>
> Before proceeding with this Chapter, write a few short paragraphs relating to a question about the social lives and experiences of young people that you would like to answer. Think about your area of interest: why are you interested in it? How would you begin to address this? What question(s)? Why do you think that this is a good or important question? Why do you wish to know the answer? What do you think the answers could be? What good could the answers lead to? For whom would the answers or the process be useful, and how? After writing answers to these questions, find one scholarly journal article from youth studies that relates to your area of interest. How does your question relate to that article?

The following section will introduce you to the praxis of youth studies via four different methodologies, sets of methods, approaches, and theories that are helping to define the field in contemporary contexts (cf. Carroll, 2006; Furlong & Cartmel, 2007; Cohen, 1999). These examples will make plain the interrelations and importance of examining assumptions, methods, and theories in relation to the study of young people.

Praxis (Linking Method and Theory First)

Beginning research in the everyday worlds of young people, especially those who are socially marginal, is one example of an epistemological approach that suggests knowledge is grounded in mutually determined discussions among people. William Carroll (2006) even goes so far as to suggest that a discipline such as youth studies could itself be *praxis*. In the conclusion to the book *Sociology for Changing the World*, Carroll recommends this:

> . . . that we view sociology itself as *praxis*. Such a critical perspective proceeds from the recognition that social life as we know it is marked by inequities that are deeply structured yet contingent features of human organization. As a systemic knowledge of the social, sociology is inevitably caught up in these inequities . . . As praxis, sociology makes a commitment to understand the deeper, systemic bases of the problems we face, whether social, psychological or ecological, which often means understanding the interconnections between allegedly separate issues and problems as in the intersections of race, class and gender that constitute lived realities. (Cited in Frampton et al., 2006: 234)

Youth studies is emerging in this way. We cannot separate assumptions and theories from the practical acts of doing research, teaching, taking care of young people, political action, and so forth; and praxis is integral to 'doing' youth studies. The ideas expressed by Carroll can be categorized as arising from interpretive and reflective epistemology, where knowledge is mutually determined by young people and others engaged in the process. Such methodologies and methods are critical in the sense that they imply that the work we do is a sort of critique, is democratic in nature, and can root out the underlying connections, issues, joys, and troubles as experienced in many contexts by youth. This new knowledge is produced in the process of praxis:

> Knowledge never floats free of its socio-political context, and if that context is organized around relations of power, then knowledge will be unavoidably implicated in those relations . . . the critic realizes that our social world . . . is not simply *given* . . . but is the result of an historical construction. It has been produced by the past actions of people and therefore *can be remade* by future actions. If this is so, then social facts can never have the same ontological status as 'facts' pertaining to natural processes that are devoid of human agency. . . . (Carroll 2004: 2 [*original emphasis*])

Carroll goes on to gather together such strategies from across various disciplines in the social sciences. Three of these approaches are of special interest for youth studies: **institutional ethnography (IE)**, **critical discourse analysis (CDA)**, and **participatory action research (PAR)**.

Institutional Ethnography

Institutional ethnography was developed by Dorothy Smith and her students. Many books and articles have been published to describe this way of doing social science (see 'List of Suggested Reading' at the end of this chapter). One relevant study that used an institutional/political ethnography is the *Ideology of 'Fag'* conducted by George Smith (1998). This paper presents an institutional ethnography in a Canadian high school and examines the social organization of homophobia as lived by young people. Smith's research revealed the myriad ways in which schools, educators, and students practise homophobia and isolate students who are not mainstream and heterosexual. The often violent and cruel ways that the word *fag* was used at school points to clear paths for intervention and action. The critical tenant of institutional ethnography is the work that goes into mapping social relations to show how the everyday experiences of young people are subjected to a host of social and ruling relations. Their personal and individual experiences of problems are then examined in the social contexts in which they arise. These social contexts are made plain through interviews, analysis of texts and documents, and/or observations. Such data is compiled into a map, which illustrates the interconnections of domination that exist and create daily problems for young people.

Critical Discourse Analysis

Related to, but also separate from, to institutional ethnography is critical discourse analysis (CDA). It is related in that it also involves the critical reading of texts that make up our social locations. It is separate in that researchers in the critical ethnographic tradition would not read texts at the level of 'discourse' but would instead examine the social processes, social organizations, and lived social practices as read in the texts: 'CDA focuses on the lens of discourse and texts that constitute our cultural environment and that come to structure our sense of self, identity and human possibility' (Carroll, 2004: 9). Examples of this work tend to be found around studies of the mass media—for example, *McLuhan's Children: The Greenpeace Message and the Media* (Dale, 1996), which outlined how media discourses were used by young people to launch effective public relations campaigns that rose to global significance. In analyzing the discourses used by Greenpeace in its media campaigns, Dale illustrates tensions within Greenpeace, which used the media effectively but also sought to criticize its use as well.

Participatory Action Research

The third strategy is participatory action research (PAR), which also holds a connection to ethnography. In some ways, it is a precursor to institutional ethnography and the principles embedded in PAR also appear in the processes of doing IE. For example, PAR also has roots in research work that attempts to understand and empower in that 'it combines social investigation, education and action designed to support those with less power in their organizational or community settings' (Hall, 2001: 171, as cited in Carroll, 2004, p. 10). Carroll places the roots of PAR in national liberation struggles and grassroots initiatives: 'In 1977, 2000 participants attended the first World Symposium on Action Research in a "quest for a new kind of scientific yet activist/emancipatory work"' (2001: 30). This approach was inspired by Paulo Freire's radical pedagogy and dialogical approach (to which we will return in Chapter 6) with the emphasis on democratic empowerment through participation in the process of research, knowledge production, and social change. These goals and ideas are similarly found and practised by those using IE—although IE has developed into a coherent process specific to mapping social and ruling relations. A quote from Dorothy Smith, the grandmother of Canadian sociology and institutional ethnography, states,

... the central project is one of inquiry which begins with issues and problems of people's lives and develops inquiry from the standpoint of their experiences in and the actualities of their everyday living. It is not, however, confined to description of local social organization or to expression of people's own experiences. Though the latter are important, indeed essential, to institutional ethnography, the sociological project is one that takes up the everyday world as a problematic for investigation. Every local setting of people's activity is permeated, organized by and contributes to social relations coordinating activities in multiple local sites. The work of the sociologist is to discover these relations and map them so that people can begin to see how their own lives and work are hooked into the lives and work of others in relations of which most of us are not aware. (2002:18)

In summary, these three critical strategies for youth studies offer research processes that can be itemized to include the following:

- Mapping and understanding many levels of influence and interconnections
- Examining how influences are socially organized through texts, observations, discussions, or images
- Examining the reproduction and resistance of social inequalities in structures and experiences such as the intersections of social class, ethnicity, region, age, and gender
- Starting from the experiences and locations of young people and their families
- Recognizing moments and possibilities of active negotiation by youth
- Taking seriously the experiential and biographical identities of youth

These critical strategies, although not always directly named, can be seen to relate to the assumptions and findings of other scholars of youth. For example, the work of Furlong and Cartmel (2007), who have posited the importance of the epistemological fallacy for youth studies (one of the follies examined in Chapter 1), holds important such relations. Their text *Young People and Social Change* illustrates how life experiences of young people in modern industrial societies have changed significantly over the past two decades. They also argue that we have come to hide the important cultural relations that impinge on young people and instead foreground certain individual levels of analyses. They are not denying the importance of understanding the individual or subjectivity and state clearly that new conceptualizations of social class must include agency and reflexivity as components of the process by which social class is reproduced in the social world. Indeed, their research shows that social class and gender continue to structure the experiences and outcomes of young people in modern contexts even though these processes (i.e., the social reproduction of inequalities by gender and social class) have become more hidden and covert.

Refining Our Critical Modes of Inquiry

The process of individualization for young people as suggested by Furlong and Cartmel demonstrates a 'progressive weakening of social bonds due to growing social diversity of life experiences' (2007: 143). They suggest that some theorists (cf. Giddens, 1976) overemphasize individual reflexivity and thus miss an important part of modernity. They are instead concerned with *not* separating subject and subjective from the real social and political contexts as a result of overestimating the extent to which individuals are able to construct their own identities:

> ... late modernity can be seen as representing a further step along
> a continuum leading from collectivized to individualized social
> identities. . . . In other words, life in high modernity revolves around
> an epistemological fallacy in which feelings of separation from the
> collectivity represent part of a long-term historical process . . . Individuals
> are forced to negotiate a set of risks which impinge upon all aspects of
> their daily lives, yet the intensification of individualism means that crises
> are perceived as individual shortcomings rather than the outcome of
> processes which are largely outside the control of individuals. (2007: 144)

In North America this idea also reverberates in the field of human development in the idea of bounded indeterminism (Fogel, Lyra, & Valsiner, 1997) which suggests that it is not unlimited agency but our reaction to what limits us that is necessary to study. Chance and change processes play an important role in limiting and providing opportunities and constraints for young people. So it is for Furlong and Cartmel as they study young people who face multiple problems and challenges but who are attempting to resolve these collective problems through individual actions while holding themselves solely responsible. While social and political landscapes have changed, young people remain tied to the class and gendered social locations, divisions, and inequalities. Some things have changed; some have remained the same so that both continuities and discontinuities require attention in youth studies:

> The experiences of young people growing up in the contemporary world
> are quite different from those encountered by earlier generations, but we
> are not convinced that recent social changes have been conceptualized
> in ways that fully enlighten us about the nature of these developments.
> Life in late modernity involves subjective discomfort and uncertainty.
> Young people can struggle to establish adult identities and maintain
> coherent biographies and may develop strategies to overcome various
> obstacles. But can their life chances still be regarded as highly structured,
> with social class and gender being critical to an understanding of
> experiences in a range of life contexts; or are we witnessing the

emergence of a 'kaleidoscope of microcultures' (McDonald, 1999: 1) that cannot be understood using conventional sociological tools and concepts? (Furlong & Cartmel, 2007: 139)

Their methods and tools are those that allow for the exposition of their central thesis and thus foreground these sources of inequality, such as social class and ethnicity, and those methods that strive to understand how young people negotiate them. This is in some ways similar to the critical strategies such as participatory action research and/or **critical ethnography** that also allow for the examination of social and political contexts, of the social networks that traditionally supported young people, and of the processes and outcomes of transitions to adulthood.

But can we use conventional social scientific tools while still needing to refine concepts such as social class and gender? Furlong and Cartmel (2007) state that late modernity's fragmentations of experiences can make such reconciliations more difficult, but biographical and narrative tools are becoming important in that they do not require the abandonment of examinations of structural inequalities in schools, communities, leisure pursuits, and so forth. They suggest that mediated experiences remain important for examination but mainly because they *distort reality*. The content of these issues of individualization and identity will be taken up again in Chapters 5 and 6, but here we notice the implications of the theory and assumptions for our research methods:

> [I]n many ways, these difficulties are being worked through very
> effectively by social scientists studying youth. The development
> of biographical perspectives, that draw on interpretations of lived
> experiences, while showing how structures are recreated both through
> actions and interpretations, offers an appropriate tool that can be used to
> understand modern life contexts. (Furlong & Cartmel, 2007: 143)

Such research is showing how the treatment of young people continues to shift with changing concepts of youth and socio-political realities such as economic and labour market demands and educational responses. Young people in contemporary contexts therefore 'have to negotiate a set of risks which were largely unknown to their parents' (Furlong & Cartmel, 2007: 1). These risks and uncertainties can be seen in their schools, families, health systems, communities, and leisure/political activities. Examining the ways in which collectivist traditions have been weakened (e.g., in the poor quality of public schooling, in youth's lack of political action, or in the inability for youth labour to be protected by unions) and individualist values have intensified is important. Furlong and Cartmel concur with Beck's (1992) conclusions relating to the weakening of collective social identities and actions. Their research into late modern societies has been characterized by other scholars as clearly demonstrating, fundamental shifts in transitions from education systems to labour markets for all young people; and extended periods of semi-dependency as many young people face delayed and disrupted transitions from their families of origin regarding domestic and housing arrangements. Furlong and Cartmel argue that the influences of peer groups and the media on young people have become increasingly powerful, and they make a strong argument against the proposition of cultural theorists . . . that style and consumption have superseded social class in shaping young people's lives. They reiterate the importance of class (and to a lesser extent gender and 'race') in structuring the forms that 'transitions to adulthood' can take for different groups of young people. (Griffen, 1997: 1)

Cohen and Ainley (2000) and others agree that the fields of social science and youth studies have taken a turn toward being too theoretical and individualistic and not grounded in the inequalities experienced by youth. Cohen's (1999) *Rethinking the Youth Question* is committed to making connections between ethnographic research and radical political work that involves young people as more than a token presence. Like others examined here, he also wants to retain an emphasis on the place of social class in shaping young people's lives. Cohen is also ambivalent about the value of postmodernism for working with young people and understanding their lives in local contexts. Cohen argues for a rejection of 'youthism', which places young people in an isolated ghetto and treats them as a different set of beings. Instead he advocates the use of cultural levels of analysis through which to think about young people's lives and the construction of their identities. The complete set of cultural nests, nested transitions, and communities of beings and practices are to be examined.

Cohen (1999) also proposes an ambitious research program concerning the genealogy of cultural codes for youth that 'focus on their function as autobiographical grammars and on the "habitus" in particular forms of family, education and labour process' (p. 180). According to Griffen (1997), the emphasis on social, cultural, psychological, and economic processes through which ethnicity, class, gender, dis/ability, and sexuality are produced and reproduced *in practice* by various groups of young people is indeed one of the major shifts in recent approaches to general social science research. This approach moves youth studies from the simplistic concern with gender or social class differences to a more dynamic place of a study of relationships between social structures and individuals. Taking up such process questions requires the study of social forces.

Cohen strives to develop such an analysis of gender and class formations in which structuralism is not lost altogether but transformed through a more interesting and critical engagement with postmodern frameworks. He does this in part by arguing for the detailed analysis of local contexts and cultural practices in relation to broader political and policy debates (see Griffen, 1997).

This argument and project is elegantly posited within the essay *In the County of the Blind: Youth Studies and Cultural Studies in Britain* (Cohen & Ainley, 2000). The authors provide a detailed history of the emergence of youth studies and cultural studies and the intersections between them. They outline, on one hand, the ways in which certain strands of cultural studies have overtheorized their work with cultural texts and lost the detailed analyses of cultural practices. On the other hand, they outline how some youth studies research has overfocused on economic and class-based types of narrow structuralism and empiricism. They concur with the argument presented in this section of the book such that youth studies and young people will remain a marginal 'sideshow' without purposeful critical attention to assumptions, methods, and processes. Cohen and Ainley provide useful directions for youth studies:

> The current complication of structural inequalities, and of the forms of self-narration through which they are actively contested and reproduced, clearly requires more sophistication and empirically grounded accounts ... If we are to do justice to what is at stake in young people's lives, we have to find new ways of integrating empirically grounded and dialogical strategies of youth research within interdisciplinary and theoretically sophisticated frameworks of comparative analysis. (2000: 242)

Similar to the other strategies reviewed in this section, Cohen and Ainley suggest the bringing together of some old and new areas of methodology arising across fields in the social sciences and humanities. Moreover, they approach the application and discussion of our new forms of knowledge that include youth-attuned and visual methods *with* and *for* young people. Indeed, this is the direction of many scholars who strive to find ways to meaningfully include young people in the conversation about youth studies (Tilleczek, 2008, 2007, 2006, 2004; Tilleczek & Hine, 2006).

Praxis (Linking Theory with Method)

This part of the chapter has a subtitle similar to the one earlier in the Chapter, but here the emphasis is on theory first, method second. This part of the Chapter will round out the previous part by presenting the work of selected scholars and theorists of youth. However, their assumptions and methods will also be made plain to further uncover the praxis and art of youth studies. The majority of textbooks relating to the study of youth continue to reduce and fragment theories of young people into biological, psychological, and social/cultural chunks. Indeed, this kind of approach itself fragments the biographies, practices, and complexities of the cultural nests within which contemporary young people live. Côté and Allahar (2006) also present theories in this manner but their inclusion of a social historical and critical outline offers value. Here I use the complex cultural nesting model to organize and critique a selection of outstanding theories and their methods.

As outlined in Chapter 1, the main elements of the complex cultural nesting model are the individual as a social being and in communities of others; multiple levels and intersections of influence and experience; the importance of the liminal areas of study; homogeneity of influences and experiences; and the social and political nature of the organized structure. In addition, the complex cultural nesting approach is preoccupied with examining processes of continuity and discontinuity (in social contexts and in youth themselves), sameness and difference, transitions and development as linear or nonlinear and iterative, and a focus on the liminal areas as locations of coming together amid practices, identities, and structures. These liminal areas hold the youth stories about being, becoming, and belonging. Not all cultural-level theories have been the same, however. As was noted earlier, many of the scholars practising youth studies are critical of solely discursive forms of postmodern cultural studies (Wyn & White, 2008; Furlong & Cartmel, 2007; Cohen, 1999). Cohen & Ainley sum this up:

> Yet, if all the world was a text and all the people in it merely quotations, some way had still to be found to tackle what was nominal outside the text but very much in the substance of what discourses of race, gender and sexuality insisted upon . . . Throughout the 1980's, cultural texts of every kind were thus laid out on the analyst's couch, not in order to be dissected according to old methods or moral anatomy (the good and important distinguished from the bad and the trivial), nor to be cured of their prosodic ills or reintegrated back into society . . . but to be taken apart around the fault lines of the unconscious identification which they provoked in the reader. . . . Yet, the cult of textuality had its downside. For one thing it failed to equip cultural studies with the intellectual tools or motivation to engage in the profound culturalization of polity and economy that was taking place during the period. . . . The deeper implications of these changes for that class structure were for a long time ignored by cultural theorists.
>
> There was an alternative tradition largely ignored in both cultural studies and mainstream youth studies, which attempted to challenge these new dichotomies and to rework the youth question in light of the larger theoretical debates, whilst at the same time struggling to create an alternative space of representation through direct interventions in the cultures of schooling, training and youth provision around issues of gender, race and class . . . In many cases, this also involved the development of a more sophisticated and reflexive approach to ethnographic work; the use of audio and video diaries, photo-mapping, story making and guided fanstasy have been variously tried as means

of developing a more dialogic and interactive approach to research with young people. (2000: 235–38)

If we begin in these liminal areas and focus our research methods and processes on the experiences of young people, on their bodies, and on their interactions in social and historical systems, then puberty and its cultural meanings and practices are of interest. Puberty has historically been solely understood in North American study as a biological event and one that creates a necessity of pathological problems for youth. As was discussed in Chapter 2, G.S. Hall in 1904 coined the term '**storm and stress**' to encapsulate the struggles of the period of adolescence. Côté and Allahar (2006) briefly trace how the biological approach was also taken up in youth psychiatry and psychology as practitioners continued only to 'treat' young people who were 'disordered'. The anti-psychiatry movement and other scholars have assisted in separating the idea of the *necessity of trouble* from the idea of youth.

Not least of these sources of challenge has arisen from the work and interpretations of cultural approaches that illustrate the nested and interwoven nature of biology, puberty, and culture. Margaret Mead's *Coming of Age in Samoa* (1928) is a classic study of female youth, puberty, and sexuality. This work is often cited as the first serious criticism of the 'storm and stress' theory and as an example of an early ethnographic work on young women. While a number of criticisms and commentaries have been offered on Mead and her work (cf. Côté 1994, 1992), contemporary fieldwork has validated the trends and helped to debunk the myth of biology as solely problematic for young people.

Indeed, Mitterauer's *History of Youth* (1993) places puberty and culture at the apex of understanding the social history of young people. He traces how in as early as 1620 the first written records appeared in which physicians 'established that peasant girls reached sexual maturity significantly later than the daughters of bourgeois and noble families' (Mitterauer, 1993: 2) and that such variability in menarche across social class was also found in 1878 in France, 1857 in Vienna, and 1860 in Germany. Moreover, the general date at which young women reach puberty is also variable over time. In some cases there are nearly four years difference reported since the first half of the 1800s such that young women are reaching sexual maturity earlier now than in the past. The cultural and historical rites of passage surrounding puberty are vital yet understudied processes for youth that open many lines of questioning.

Where are current North American rites of passage? What do we do in our communities and societies in the liminality that keep young people dependent for ever-increasing years? Cultural psychology is another example of theory that attends to the liminal areas within cultural nests. The new move in North America toward 'positive youth development' has emerged from the field of human development and developmental psychology as a coming together with cultural psychology and the sociological focus on context, action, advocacy, and policy.

Critical Thinking Activities

1. Propose a question that you would like to ask about the lives, experiences, and social contexts of youth. What is the question, why is it a 'good' one, and how would you begin to think about answering it? Are you using a praxis approach? Explain.
2. Compare and contrast two theories of youth, and state which one is the most useful for the emergence of youth studies. How does each theory proceed with methods for doing research? What are the applications of each?
3. Watch the segments of the *Merchants of Cool* (see List of Suggested Websites, below) that are related to doing market research on young people (hint: they use focus groups and ethnography). They use these methods of social science in their work but who is this research for? What good comes of this work for young people?
4. Revisit the Margaret Mead site given in the List of Suggested Websites with the goal of wanting to understand Mead's theory, her methods, and criticisms of her work. What does this suggest about the relationships between puberty and culture?

Further Readings

Carroll, W. (2004). *Critical Strategies for Social Research*. Toronto: Canadian Scholars' Press.

Mead, M. (1928). Anuik's 2008 review of the book points out that the work well demonstrates *Coming of Age in Samoa*. New York: W. Morrow and Company.

Smith, D. (2002). Institutional ethnography. In T. May (Ed.). *Qualitative Research in Action*. Thousand Oaks, CA: Sage Publications.

Schwandt. (2007). *Dictionary of Qualitative Inquiry* (3rd Ed.). Los Angeles: Sage Publications.

Suggested Websites

Margaret Mead site
http://www.loc.gov/exhibits/mead/field-samoa.html

Merchants of Cool
http://www.pbs.org/wgbh/pages/frontline/shows/cool/view/

Chapter Four

Can There Be a Social Science *with* and *for* Youth?

Introduction

Before proceeding to directly answer this question, it is useful to stop and examine some sources of data that begin to illustrate the realities and structures of the lives and times of contemporary young people. Certainly, this is only one kind of data, and some gaps will be filled throughout the book. These later chapters will provide further information on social contexts, practices, processes of reproduction, and acts of negotiation/resistance in contexts such as schools, families, communities, peer groups, politics, mass media, and so forth.

Conducting research to answer some of the broadest questions about the well-being of young people requires setting clear directions. If we take seriously the need to understand the complex cultural nests arising from such a broad view, the following questions are some that could be posed:

1. What are the trends and issues faced by contemporary youth?
2. What are the main stumbling points for youth and for whom do they most often exist?
3. What are the processes and mechanisms by which problems and inequalities are organized?
4. How can/do young people actively negotiate societal and personal challenges?
5. How can/do practitioners and researchers become engaged in better means of researching and supporting well-being for young people, as young people define it for themselves?
6. What do practitioners understand about young people and how do they act on this knowledge?

This chapter addresses questions 1 and 2 by moving toward a synthesis of the existing statistical data, evaluating that data critically, and continuing to ponder how we can best design research to examine the processes by which these data trends and disparities are organized. It is precisely this in-depth knowledge that is so often missing from the field of youth studies but that is essential for innovations in policy and practice *with* and *for* young people. However, it is not sufficient to end our investigations with these larger trends as discussed here. We will also endeavour to know why and how these trends have come to be so, what they say about young people's experience, and what can be done to address and alter them. The dearth of this kind of in-depth knowledge suggests that young people remain subject to numerical **marginalization** (Qvortrup, 2001). The goal of this kind of inquiry is to continue to create, add to, and mobilize knowledge to enable good lives for Canada's young people, while also learning all we can about the best ways to conduct research *with* and *for* them.

This chapter begins with some general trends and patterns and reflects on the meaning of the data. Next, the chapter presents current evidence of the social and political realities that make up the cultural nests of contemporary youth and that facilitates or negates youth's being, becoming, and belonging.

Current Global and Canadian Contexts

Worldwide bodies of statistical inquiry support the presence of inequalities and the maldistribution of developmental health for young people. Globally, the World Health Organization (2003), UNICEF, United Nations, UNCESCO, and the Organisation for Economic and Co-operative Development (OECD)'s Programme for International Student Assessment (PISA) provide excellent sources of data. The World Health Organization (WHO) defines *health* as 'a state of complete physical, mental and social well-being and not merely the absence of disease or infirmity' (WHO, 1946). This definition identifies health as a positive entity, which suggests that the absence of disease by itself does not necessarily mean that a young person is healthy. While this classic definition has not been amended since 1946, a 2003 WHO document on *Strategic Directions for Improving the Health and Development of Children and Adolescents* identifies several health indicators: maternal and newborn health, nutrition, communicable diseases, injuries and violence, physical environment, adolescent health, and psychosocial health and development. The document and data from WHO show evidence of the absolute deterioration in the health of young people such that 'most of the unfinished health agenda at the doorstep of the 21st century is due to inadequate efforts to address childhood illness' (WHO, 2003: 5) as stated in these broad and inclusive terms.

These faltering youth outcomes exist within 'modernity's paradox' in which massive expansion in global wealth generation exists alongside growing incidences of health deterioration, especially for those already marginalized by social class, gender, region, ethnicity, and age (Keating & Hertzman, 1999).

This marginalization takes place at precisely the same time that developmental needs for inclusion and empowerment become present for young people. Two constellations of threats to youth can be categorized and examined in the data.

The first constellation of threats to young people on global and national levels is the presence of the risk society (Beck, 1992) as characterized by an eradication of social networks, such as families and secure employment; a set of risks and uncertainties, such as high unemployment; and an increasingly burdened public school system. These trends place increasing pressures on families and reduce the possibility of secure income and the provision of optimal care, especially for those living in poverty (Ross & Wu, 1995). These unsettled social contexts, including parental unemployment, result in youth transitions through secondary school, which are becoming increasingly difficult to negotiate (Furlong & Cartmel, 2007; Tilleczek & Lewko, 2001) and especially so for young people marginalized by social class, ethnicity, and region (Tilleczek, 2008b, c). Keating and Mustard (1993: 88) conclude that '[a]lthough economically poor families are at the highest risk of this form of family insecurity, the changes we are currently experiencing are so widespread that negative consequences are occurring even for the families of children that are moderately secure economically'. These trends are explored further, and in greater detail, in Chapter 6.

A second and related constellation of threats to youth is a further result of the expansion of capital taking primacy over the needs of the environment, land, and young people (McNally, 2002) with an offshoot observed in the pervasive and growing culture of commodification and consumption and the deterioration of the environment. Do young people now value money over freedom? What does this mean, especially for youth who have access to media technology and paid work, and whose lives are gated into low-paid 'McJobs' and mass consumption of the latest US invention? Young people are purchasing ever-changing fashion, music, and technologies (Latham 2002), yet current evidence suggests that the more young people engage in consumer culture, the greater can be their feelings of isolation on one hand, and connection on the other (Latham, 2002; Schor, 2004). These trends will be examined in detail in Chapter 5 when we turn to a discussion of modern youth at work and play. At this point, it is sufficient to point out the intricacies and connections among levels of social and political analysis that require attention and to take a look at a selection of research that has examined these intricate social connections.

Nationally, numerous Canadian researchers including Keating and Hertzman (1999) and Willms (2002, 2009) have analyzed the abundance of statistical evidence regarding these disparities by age, region, ethnicity, gender, and social class. Many provinces, such as Manitoba, are also accumulating powerful statistical evidence by bringing together multiple data sets. The growing and diverse body of global, national, and provincial statistical data on childhood and youth is too abundant to name here (see the 'List of Suggested Readings' at the end of the chapter). It is vital to know statistically, for example, that poverty remains a critical factor relating to school failure, that Aboriginal youth face multiple social risks, and that the main cause of death for young men is motor vehicle accidents (Tilleczek, 2006). And yet equally important to note is that not all poor youth fail in school, that many Aboriginal youth are incredibly resilient, and that not all young people drive erratically or injure themselves. Such nuances and dichotomies are the kinds of material that require further examination.

Keating and Hertzman (1999: 1) attest to the fact that there is 'troubling scientific evidence that points to a societal breakdown in the process of making human beings human. The signs of this breakdown are seen in growing rates of alienation, apathy . . . and violence we have observed in youth . . . in recent decades'. In their work with the Canadian Institute for Advanced Research (Keating & Hertzman, 1999), a group of researchers from diverse scientific disciplines have provided evidence of decline, especially for the most vulnerable young people: 'In particular, labour market policies that do not recognize the extensive demands of families with young children, combined with the dearth of good affordable child care, create a situation in which adequate nurturing of the next generation cannot be assured' (Keating & Mustard, 1993: 88).

Youth Trends in Communities, at Work, and in Families

The Canadian Council of Social Development's (2006) *The Progress of Canada's Children & Youth* (www.ccsd.ca/pccy/2006/) has reported on two constellations of data trends for youth. In regard to labour market trends, access to paid work remains a major factor in young people's lives in Canada. More than one in five (23 per cent) young teens aged 14 and 15 in 2000 said they had worked for an employer in the previous week, up from 16 per cent in 1998. Forty-eight per cent said they had worked for pay at odd jobs (up from 36 per cent in 1998), 14 percent had worked at a family business, and 18 per cent had worked without pay. When asked what kind of job they had worked at most in the previous week, odd jobs came out on top (CCSD, 2006). The CCSD (2006) also reported that in 2000, more than three-quarters (77 per cent) of teens aged 14 and 15 received money from their parents in the previous week, with 70 per cent receiving $40 or less per week. Youth in low-income families were just as likely as those in higher income families to receive money from their parents, but they were less likely to receive money from an employer (20 per cent compared to 24 per cent) or from odd jobs (36 per cent and 43 per cent, respectively).

In fact, most Canadian youth aged 15 to 24 were in the paid labour force—68 per cent in 2004, up from 64 per cent in 1994. However, one out of every three unemployed workers was a young person, and the youth unemployment rate is double that of the adult rate. This suggests that young people comprise a 'yo-yo' workforce in Canada—used when necessary and retracted when inconvenient or when the labour market fluctuates. This unemployment rate is also higher than the rate for adults aged 25 to 44—despite the fact that young people today are more highly educated than at any other point in Canadian history (CCSD, 2006). Young adults have fared somewhat better than teens in terms of unemployment but still had an unemployment rate of 10.3 per cent in 2004, virtually unchanged since 2000.

Health Canada (2006) reported that most youth had a happy home life in 2001, but this decreased as they got older. The study also found that both boys and girls confide more easily in their mothers than in their fathers, a fact that also declines with age for both genders. By grade 10, in fact, 15 per cent fewer girls said they were happy with their lives at home than was the case in grade 6. The majority of students across the grades felt trusted by their parents, valued what their parents thought of them, and desired parental approval. Again, these feelings declined with age. More boys than girls in grades 6 to 10 said they were understood by their parents. Older girls—those in grades 8 and 10—were less likely to say their parents understood and trusted them. They were less satisfied with their home life, had more arguments, and had more desire to leave home. Health Canada (2006) also reported that grade 10 students who had a more positive relationship with their parents were more likely to be satisfied with their lives. Chapter 6 zooms in on these trends in youth–parent relationships and details processes that occur in the home.

The cultural nests for youth also extend outside the family and into the community. The civic vitality of communities includes,

> the value placed on children and the people who value them, the expectations for the future—both for the children themselves and for the larger community—and levels of collective support which focus on or include children. A vital community is one which provides young people with opportunities to grow and develop to their full potential; it encourages them to participate in local initiatives, and advocates on their behalf. (CCSD, 2006: 43)

This concept is more easily identified than enacted. Formal political engagement is often used as a proxy measure of youth engagement and most often we know only about formal voting behaviour. We will unpack this further in Part 4 and look at ways to think about *informal* engagement and acts of resistance. In Chapter 8 we examine the formal voting from the June 2004 federal election, which was the first opportunity for those young people who were 18 years of age at that time to vote. Statistics show that 39 per cent of them did so, according to the Canadian Council on Development (CCD, 2006). However, the chief electoral officer of Canada warned that these results could not be compared to other elections due to differences in methodologies

---

Box 4.1 Student Vote

Visit the website of Student Vote (www.studentvote.ca/). Read the information on what Student Vote is, what it does, its philosophy, and how its
program works. Embedded in this information are a number of results from
past student elections in Canada. What kinds of trends do you observe? Is
this program poised to make a difference in the democratic engagement of
Canadian youth? Explain your position.

---

of vote counting. He believed that low voter turnout among youth had not
necessarily been resolved even though close to 40 per cent of youth cast votes
in that one election. Youth were still being seen as marginal to the political
landscape of Canada. Certainly, the 2007 federal election did not help matters
with its insistence on photo ID at the polls since so many young people do
not yet have valid government photo ID. Young people in Canada continue
to vote at rates nearly 35 points lower than adults aged 57 and older (CCSD,
2006). Studies of the 1993, 1997, and 2000 federal elections found that age
was the strongest predictor of voter turnout: young people were less likely
than older Canadians to vote, and their voting rate was declining over time.
Between 1990 and 1998, the reported voter turnout dropped significantly—
from 88 per cent to 81 per cent—with most of the decline occurring among
young people (CCSD, 2006).

However, young people are active in community and politics in other ways.
Between 1996/97 and 2003, there was a 41 per cent increase in the participation of youth aged 15 to 19 as members of voluntary organizations or
associations. Among young adults aged 20 to 24, the increase was 39 per cent,
and for adults over age 25, their participation in community groups rose
by 16 per cent. Young women were more likely than men to participate in
voluntary organizations or associations, and the increase in young women's
participation rate exceeded that of men (CCSD, 2006). One explanation for
increases in this kind of volunteerism is the inclusion of 'community hours'
as required for graduation from high school in many provinces. Moreover,
scholarships for universities are progressively moving toward the evaluation
of community service as well as academic achievement. There is also a claim
that engagement of young people in the democratic process will inspire and
incite them toward political participation and voting. Indeed, *Student Vote*
is one Canadian program that is 'a non-profit, non-partisan organization
working with educators to engage young Canadians in the democratic process'
(Student Vote Website, see Box 4.1).

Global and Local Youth Trends: An Example from Aboriginal Canada

The United Nations Convention on the Rights of the Child is currently being used as an analytical tool to examine the many contraventions that are occurring for Aboriginal youth and communities in Canada (cf. Blackstock, Clarke, Cullen, et al., 2004; Tilleczek, 2008e).

> The lived experience of Aboriginal children and youth in Canada
> continues to be predominated by social exclusion, discrimination
> and oppression. The significant body of evidence regarding the
> disproportionate risk faced by Aboriginal children has been inadequate
> to motivate the actions needed to move them out of the categories of
> marginalized, at risk and vulnerable. Nor has it promoted substantial
> internal reflection within social work or other helping professions on
> what our role has been in perpetrating the harm and our concordant
> responsibility to understand and reconcile the harm . . . To get there we
> must collectively make loud the legislation, values, regulations, systems
> and actions that perpetuate colonization and its concordant impacts
> on Aboriginal children and their families including those harmful and
> colonial philosophies and practices that are embedded in social work
> itself. It means understanding the harm from those who experienced it,
> it means setting aside the instinct to rationalize it or to turn away from
> it because it is too difficult to hear—or we feel blamed. It means having
> conversations about some of the basic values and beliefs that shape our
> concepts of what social work is. It means working with, versus working
> for, Aboriginal peoples. . . . (Blackstock, 2009: 36)

Indeed, a close read of the trends and the Convention demonstrate the many ways in which Canada's Aboriginal youth rights are not protected. These national-level trends point to real and ongoing injustices inhabiting the daily lives and well-being of Canada's Aboriginal youth. In 2001, according to the Canadian Community Health Survey, the off-reserve Aboriginal population had lower levels of household income and educational attainment and was less likely to have worked the entire year than the non-Aboriginal population (Tjepkema, 2002). For example, 44 per cent of Aboriginal persons (25 and older) in Canada—48 per cent in rural areas—had not graduated from secondary school. The percentage for the non-Aboriginal population was 23 per cent, and 32 per cent in rural areas.

The First Nations Regional Longitudinal Health Survey (RHS) conducted in Canada was first conducted in 2002–03 by the First Nations Information Governance Committee (now referred to as the First Nations Information Governance Centre) and was repeated in 2008–10. First Nation youth populations living on-reserve and in northern First Nations communities across Canada. In so doing, the RHS succinctly reported the following:

Fair/poor overall health was a good predictor of non-attendance at
school, of learning problems, and of not liking school. The induced
peer/societal precursors to reduced school performance, especially as
related to nonattendance and repeat grades, are related to increased
alcohol consumption, smoking and sexual activity among older youth.
Diet was found to be an important indicator of school performance
among First Nations youth. Always eating a nutritious, balanced diet is
associated with lower rates of grade repetition, less learning problems,
and higher rates of liking school very much (as compared to never).
Participating in sports and frequency of physical activity are also
positively associated with attending school. Relationships between
residential schools, traditional language and culture, and learning
problems at school were also found to be present in the data. (RHS,
2003: 159)

In terms of poverty, 27 per cent of Aboriginal households in 2001 had a low
household income compared to 10 per cent for non-Aboriginal households. In
addition, 38 per cent of Aboriginal persons (ages 15 to 75) worked the entire
year compared to 53 per cent of the non-Aboriginal population. In 2001, Hull
stated that the majority of Aboriginal youth lived in low-income families
(based on the Statistics Canada definition of *low-income*).

The First Nations Regional Longitudinal Health Survey (2003) further
reports that over half (57.4 per cent) of the youth living in First Nations
communities lived in households with six or more people, mostly family. About
one-third (32.4 per cent) lived with more than two adults, and half lived with
four or more children and youth. The number of household members ranged
from 1 to 26, with a mean of 6.6. Community size and relative isolation appear
to be related to family and housing situations, and to the degree of value
assigned to First Nations languages and cultures. Youth in small communities
(<300 residents) reported lower levels of crowding than those in large communities (>1,500 residents):

Abundant connections to family, community and nation were reported
by youth living in First Nations communities. A significant proportion
of these youth reported living in homes with their extended families and
expressed preferences for First Nations languages and, to some extent,
traditional cultural events. Cultural influences came from many sources
in the family and community. At the same time, the youth were less
fluent in the language of their First Nation than in English or French.
About half of the youth did not value participating in traditional cultural
events. Despite being richly surrounded by extended family households,
some youth lived in overcrowded conditions that could have negative
implications for mental and physical health and overall well-being. (RHS
2003: 153)

Diabetes and suicide remain critical youth health issues in Aboriginal communities (Tilleczek, 2008b). But the RHS (2003) reported that over all in their youth sample 57.2 per cent considered themselves to be in very good or excellent health, 32.9 per cent rated their health as good, and only 9.9 per cent reported their health as fair or poor. Unpublished data provided by the federal Office for Disability Issues (ODI) and reported in the RHS (2003) indicates that disability is 1.5 times more prevalent among First Nations children from birth to 14 years than among non-Aboriginal children in Canada. However, at 3.5 per cent, the reported prevalence of learning disability among First Nations youth is not as high as in the general population, where 6.3 per cent of youths have this condition. Lesser access by First Nations youth to diagnosis of learning disability by educational psychologists and other professionals may be a factor that accounts for some of the reported difference. Only 12.6 per cent of First Nations youth with learning disability are receiving interventions to address this condition (RHS, 2003). Indeed, fully 48.6 per cent and 27.8 per cent of First Nation youth report having difficulty in math and reading, respectively (RHS, 2003).

Speaking a First Nations language was considered important by most of the youth surveyed in the RHS (82.1 per cent), and having traditional cultural events in one's life was considered important by about half of the youth (54.8 per cent). The actual daily use of First Nations languages by youth lags behind the sense of importance youth place on speaking it (only 13.9 per cent of the youth surveyed reported actually using a First Nations language daily). The majority of those who did report speaking daily in a First Nations language spoke *only* First Nations languages (12.6 per cent of the total surveyed, compared with the 13.9 per cent who reported speaking a First Nations language daily). However, approximately three times as many youth *understood* a First Nations language fluently or relatively well (32.8 per cent). In contrast, 87.6 per cent of respondents use English (85.4 per cent), French (2.4 per cent), or American Sign Language (ASL) as their language of daily use (RHS, 2003).

Injury rates are higher in youth than in any other age group globally and in Canada (Tilleczek, 2006), and the Regional Health Survey (RHS, 2003) results show that First Nations youth are at much greater risk than other youth in Canada. The most common causes of injury in First Nations youth were falls, sports, motor vehicle crashes, and bicycle accidents. Higher rates were found for First Nations males and for First Nation with personal problems, such as depression, low self-esteem, problems in learning at school, recent loss of someone close due to suicide, and drinking (RHS, 2003).

A Royal Commission (Chenier, 1995) report on suicide among Aboriginal people suggests that as many as 25 per cent of accidental deaths among Aboriginal people are actually unreported suicides. Those people who identified themselves as Aboriginal (off-reserve only) in the Community Health Survey were three times more likely to have seriously considered committing suicide when compared to their non-Aboriginal counterparts. Between January 1, 2001, and July 30, 2001, 16 youth suicides were recorded on 49 northern Ontario reserves. In the previous year—2000—there were 26 such deaths (Adlaf & Paglia, 2001). Rates of suicide among First Nations youth are estimated to be five to six times higher than the national average for non-Aboriginal youth (RHS, 2003). Some communities have shown disturbing trends of suicide rates that continue to increase over time. Among the Nishnawbe Aski youth in northern Ontario, the number of completed suicides increased an incredible 400 per cent over a 10-year period from 5 in 1986 to 25 in 1995 (cited in RHS, 2003).

The implication derived has been that regional or geographical remoteness may be the most critical factor in these rates. But Chandler and Lalonde's (1998; 2008) work with First Nations youth and communities in British Columbia shows an important contradiction. They found higher rates of suicide for youth living in urban settings (147.4 per 100,000 population) as compared to youth living in either rural (95.1 per 100,000) or remote (78.2 per 100,000) settings. Chandler and Lalonde's research is critical and encouraging because it begins to describe factors and circumstances that communities may gain control over and that may be protective against suicide. For the British Columbia population, clear evidence of an inverse relationship between rates of First Nations youth suicide and 'cultural continuity' was found. Cultural continuity is a concept that relates to a state of overall community wellness. The study defined it as the community being involved in some aspects of (1) self-government, (2) land claims, (3) control over its educational system, (4) health services, (5) police/fire services; or (6) having cultural facilities available for use by members. Communities that had more of the factors present—higher levels of cultural continuity—also showed lower rates of suicide among their youth. Rates of suicide in communities without any of these protective factors were 138 per 100,000 population versus 0 per 100,000 population for those with all six factors present (Chandler & Lalonde, 2008).

Toward Youth Studies *with* and *for* Young People

If we take seriously the trends examined so far and the evidence of ongoing struggles and joys experienced by homogenous communities of Canadian youth, questions arise about what more we need to know, how should we come to know it, and how can we move forward in a youth studies *with* and *for* young people.

In using a complex cultural nesting approach, theory and research is conducted as praxis for examining the lives and conditions of youth and potentially enhancing the practice of researchers, practitioners, parents, and community members. A continuous loop of knowledge-making and discussion occurs and is built into the design, methods, and strategies of research.

Currents arising from subaltern studies (cf. Apple & Buras, 2006), critical 'praxicological' social inquiry (Carroll, 2004), and voiced research (cf. Smyth & Hattam, 2001) are adapted so as to speak to, listen to (and actually hear), and respond to young people. The goal is to continue to generate and mobilize knowledge to enable successes for Canada's young people while also learning all we can about the best ways to conduct research *with* and *for* them. But will this in fact make a difference? Is it possible to have a social science *with* and *for* youth? If so, what does it look like?

In keeping with the health and educational trends of Aboriginal youth in Canada, how do we move forward to understand the daily lives, experiences, outcomes, social contexts, and influences on this situation? What would a social science with and for youth look like if we were to practise it in relation to these issues? Box 4.2 outlines a current Canadian situation that requires study and action. In coming to understand the lives, struggles, and joys of the people of the community of Attawapiskat, how might we best proceed with this kind of social science? What would the elements of the research process look like?

Parts One and Two of the book have aimed to provide an examination and synthesis of the need to know the political, social, and historical assumptions underlying the practice or treatment of youth. We have learned from many others in relation to how they approach their work to better inform this treatment. What are the main lessons and correspondences in this work? What are the main tensions and foci needed to move ahead? What do these look

---

Box 4.2 Youth Struggles, Resistance, and Rights in Attawapiskat, Ontario

This site (www.attawapiskat-school.com/Home.html) has gathered together much information pertaining to a youth rights movement in Canada. As such, it addresses the ways in which the UN Convention on the Rights of the Child has been contravened. The story of Attawapiskat also details how the young people, their community, and thousands of other youth and adults in Canada are rallying around this Aboriginal community that has no school. This site outlines the social, political, and experiential aspects of this story. For example, you will find YouTube coverage of the debates in the Canadian House of Commons, and information from the conference held in Toronto in 2008. In reading through this information, imagine how you would begin to enact a social science *with* and *for* youth. Where would you start? What questions would need to be asked? What strategies would you use?

like? What do the scholars, theorists, and their methods teach us about youth studies?

In general, there has been an important move toward a discussion of the messy in-between that is the *being* of youth. This discussion takes seriously the lives and times of young people and studies them as indicators of the wellness of modern societies. However, the meanings of the liminality of youth, the lack of consideration of the humanities and arts, and the continued adult-centric nature of social science should be further examined. The tensions of *being, becoming*, and *belonging* must be considered both within and across the range of cultural nests. As Lee (1998) suggests, we need to move toward embracing an immature social science that allows for the recognition and privileging of the unfinished and incomplete aspects of people and contexts. Chapters 3 and 4 have provided some points of departure in moving this work ahead. These include the following concepts:

1. Attending to voiced and youth-attuned research through the use of critical strategies for social research.
2. Attending to an action and social justice orientation *with* and *for* young people.
3. Attending to the level and scope of our work with attentions guided toward the study of youth experiences, social structures, cultural processes, and praxis for youth studies.
4. Attending to diversity, homogeneity, and inequality in the study of youth.
5. Attending to social history and the representations/treatment of youth.
6. Animating, sharing, and discussing the work in conversations with those who are invested—and those who are not!

Critical Thinking Activities

1. Revisit your proposed question that you would like to ask about the lives, experiences, and social contexts of youth. Would you alter this question now? Would you go about answering it the same way? How does your proposed work move toward a social science with and for young people? Explain.
2. How should young people themselves be engaged in a social science *with* and *for* youth? What is our place in the process of engaging them? Could it make any difference to them? Explain.
3. Visit the websites noted in the List of Suggested Websites, below. At each site (other than for the Student Vote Site), find a report related to the cultural nests and contemporary contexts of young people. Read the executive summary and comment on the main findings of the research. Comment also on the ways in which the researchers conducted their work with particular attention to their methods. For example, did they use questionnaires from a survey, experiments, and/or ethnographic research? If you were conducting

research on youth, what would you be interested in studying? How would you approach it? Refer back to Chapter 3 on the praxis of youth studies and consider how you would do this work *with* and *for* young people or how the work could be applied to assist youth.

Further Readings

Smyth & Hattam. (2001). 'Voiced' research as a sociology for understanding dropping out of school. *British Journal of the Sociology of Education, 22*, 401–15.

Suggested Websites

Canadian Council on Social Development (*The Progress of Canada's Children and Youth, 2006*) www.ccsd.ca/pccy/2006/

First Nations Regional Longitudinal Health Survey
www.rhs-ers.ca/english/

International Childhood and Youth Research Network
www.icyrnet.net/

National Longitudinal Survey of Children and Youth
www.statcan.gc.ca/cgi-bin/imdb/p2SV.pl?Function=getSurvey&SDDS=
4450&lang=en&db=imdb&adm=8&dis=2

Student Vote Site
www.studentvote.ca/

UNICEF (UN Convention on the Rights of the Child)
www.unicef.org

World Health Organization (WHO)
www.who.int/en

Part Three

The Remains of the Everyday: Influences and Negotiations

The manner in which contemporary young people work and play requires a thorough discussion of one of the most significant influences on their lives: modern technologies, in particular the screen technologies that have arisen in contemporary digital culture. Part Three of this book provides a context for the work and play of contemporary young people by focusing on their immersion in technology and its pervasive influence. We argue that all too often this kind of examination is missing or made trite by research. Young people are not offered a space to enhance understandings and make critical statements about the modern context's influence upon them.

By way of context, Part Three examines the nature of the modern project in relation to the lives of contemporary young people. We argue that one of the principal ambitions of the modern project is an unprecedented betterment of the human condition. The insights emerging from the natural sciences encouraged that ambition by creating the impression that the nagging problems of human imperfection were not permanent features of existence but temporary historical conditions open to human intervention and change. Modernity aspired to remake the world in a way that would ameliorate or eliminate those conditions in order to free human life from two of its most stubborn problems: human suffering and death. It is critical to recognize that modern technology was born in the womb of that aspiration. Our digital cultures, the Internet, computers, and biotechnologies are the direct descendants of the modern desire to transform the human and nonhuman worlds in this way (Fukuyama, 2000).

As a rule all human inquiry and action aims to improve human life in some measure. In that respect there is no difference between ancient and modern technology. However, it does not follow from this similarity that there is no difference of any kind between ancient and modern technologies or between the ambitions on which they rest. One way of exploring the differences between them is through a comparison of ancient Greek notions of history and Christian and modern apocalyptic thinking. The ancient Greeks had a concept of history, even linear history, but for them whatever improvements were possible within that history were also subject to forces of decay that were themselves considered to be permanent features of human life (Camus, 1991). What this meant was that for the Greeks no social or personal order, however sound or desirable, was ever free from the counterinfluence of chaos that would prevent its perfect realization and set a limit to its endurance in time. Christian and modern apocalyptic thinking broke with the ancient world on this basic point and in doing so set the stage for a belief in a type of technological progress that was in principle unlimited because it was bound by no substantial counterforce (Cohn, 1995). In this respect several contemporary authors have made compelling cases for the apocalyptic origins of both revolutionary movements and the liberal bourgeois effort to achieve technical mastery of human and nonhuman nature (Camus, 1991; Voegelin, 1990; Grant, 1969). More recently Jean Baudrillard (cf. 1996) has explained the manner in which this ambition has played itself out in modern digital and computer technologies. This is one of the strands we follow in Chapter 5.

Understanding the role of young people in the advent of modern digital technologies is an important and difficult question. As we argue in this chapter, young people are certainly among the primary consumers of these technologies, and therefore provide a significant impetus for their creation. It is also true that because young people are relative newcomers to the world and so are not bound entirely by what has gone before them, they introduce a kind of novelty into the world that is a powerful engine of social, personal, and technological change. As Hannah Arendt has argued, it is one of the central features of human natality that 'with each birth something uniquely new comes into the world' (Arendt, 1958). The importance of this insight notwithstanding, we should be wary of emphasizing human natality and the uniqueness of youth to the point of obscuring from view the notion of human sameness and thereby suggesting that young people are by nature responsible for the advent of modern technology. Human uniqueness is not absolute, and therefore the fact of natality by itself does not explain the modern desire for a form of technological change that is both unique and unprecedented. To state this another way, the novelty of youth is always balanced by the constants of the human condition. Youth cannot supply the motivation necessary for a form of novel technology. Some other influence is required for this notion to gain credence.

The theme of Chapter 5 centres around the idea that modern youth are deeply embedded in an essentially technological society that shapes their lives in a variety of ways and that is manifest in a host of secondary phenomena that are parasitic—consumer cultures that hold young people captive in cycles of consuming ever newer and greater numbers of items, capitalist organizations of labour, and the disappearance of public spaces. As has been argued in Parts One and Two of this book, these situations create layers of culture for young people that require careful examination.

Chapter 6 builds on this analysis of modern contexts by examining the impact of technology on the organization of youth's central cultural nests of public education, schools, families, and friendships. This chapter asks, what is the character of the relationships that young people now have within their homes, schools, and communities? How has this been organized in modern society? And what does this mean for the way youth live their daily lives in modern society?

Chapter Five

Modern Youth at Work and Play*

The vampire is literally an insatiable consumer driven by hunger for perpetual youth, while the cyborg has incorporated the machineries of consumption into its juvenescent flesh. Indeed, the conspicuous unnaturalness of both figures, their frankly mutant character, serves to point out how deeply youth has come to be defined by its ensnarement in the norms and ideologies of consumption rather than by more conventional measures of identity rooted in the structures of family life. The vampire and the cyborg thus provide fruitful models for apprehending the forms of cultural activity—for labour and leisure— that contemporary capitalist society has staked out for youth, offering a potent mediation on the promises and perils inherent in youth consumption. (Latham, 2002: 1)

In our view, trends in leisure highlight the ways in which the epistemological fallacy of late modernity is sustained. The blurring of class and gender divisions in leisure, which largely arise from processes of commercialization, helps to create an illusion of individuality and classlessness. Social identities are partly shaped through lived experiences in the related spheres of leisure and consumption and any apparent weakening of class divisions in these fields will therefore manifest in the ways in which people subjectively locate themselves in the social world. (Furlong & Cartmel, 2007: 71)

---

*Chapter 5 and the introduction to Part Three were co-written with Ron Srigley of the University of Prince Edward Island and the author of *Eric Voegelin's Platonic Theology*. Ron is also the translator of *Albert Camus, Christian Metaphysics and Neoplatonism*. His latest book, *Greece in Rags: Albert Camus' Critique of Modernity*, is forthcoming.

Introduction: The Life of Leisure? Youth's Technological Consumption

The extent of technology's influence on young people is immediately apparent to any observer of youth culture. Many young people access high-speed satellite and wireless Internet technologies daily, post to YouTube, use cellphones, text-message, play video games, use email or MSN, download music, and use social/semantic networking programs and processes (e.g., Facebook, MySpace, Twitter, chat rooms) to mediate their relationships with family and friends. In fact, there has been an enormous increase in the past five years in media use among young people:

> Five years ago, we reported that young people spent an average of nearly 6.5 (6.21) hours a day with media—and managed to pack more than 8.5 hours (8.33) worth of media content into that time by multitasking. At that point it seemed that young people's lives were filled to the bursting point with media. Today, however, those levels of use have been shattered. Over the last five years, young people have increased the time they spend consuming media by an hour and seventeen minutes daily, from 6.21 to 7.38—almost the amount of time most adults spend
> at work each day, except that young people use media seven days a week instead of five . . . Today they pack a total of 10 hours and 25 minutes worth of media content into those 7.5 hours. (Kaiser Foundation, 2010: 2)

In addition to these technologically driven activities, young people also purchase the gadgets and machines necessary to engage in these activities. Young people use a significant portion of their wealth to buy the artifacts of technology, such as MP3 players, gaming consoles, cellphones, and computers. The principal consequence of this access is that young people annually listen to thousands of hours of music and watch an almost immeasurable amount of reality television programming, YouTube videos, and Hollywood movies. In addition to these leisure activities, young people also work in jobs that are both fast-paced and geared toward technological efficiency. The net result of this experience is that by the time a contemporary young person has reached the age of 15, her direct experience of life has been subordinated to the narratives of thousands of situational comedies, hundreds of films, thousands of websites and chat rooms, and innumerable advertisements, all offering ever more powerful enticements to consume. As Beder (2009) argues, the corporate capture of childhood and youth has come from multiple sources in business and marketing, and has tentacles that have firmly spread into homes, schools, and the head spaces of modern leisure hours.

The most recent trends in the use of digital technology among North American young people support Beder's claim. In fact, young Canadians are now among the most wired in the world (Media Awareness Network, 2006: 8). The speed with which technology has entered North American youth cultures is astonishing, and has grown exponentially in recent years. In 2003, 55 per cent of all Canadian households had at least one family member who regularly used the Internet at home—up from 29 per cent in 1999. As of 2003, Internet use was highest in British Columbia, Ontario, and Alberta, where approximately 6 out of every 10 households were connected to the Internet (Canadian Council on Social Development, 2006). According to Ipsos Reid (2004) almost half of young people (aged 12 to 17) said they used the Internet every day or several times a week for research projects or homework, and 73 per cent said they used the Internet for email either every day or a few times a week. Almost half (48 per cent) used chat rooms daily, while another 29 per cent chatted several times a month. These young people felt that they could have 'real-time' and living conversations with several people at once via chat rooms. According to a study by the Media Awareness Network (2001), 60 per cent of Canadian youth (aged 9 to 17) have used chat rooms at some point. As age increased, so did the likelihood of accessing them. Of those who had used chat rooms, 85 per cent said they chatted unsupervised from their homes and 43 per cent said they had encountered someone on the Internet who had requested personal information about them (e.g., a photograph, a phone number, or an address); close to half (46 per cent) said that someone had made unwanted sexual comments to them while in a chat room. New Phase II data is now out from the Media Awareness Network to update its original 2001 study:

> One of the most interesting changes we discovered was in the way parents and children now see the Net. Parents' hopeful belief that a home computer would give their children a leg up in school seems long gone. The mothers and fathers we talked to in Edmonton, Toronto and Montreal in 2003 almost universally complained that their children are wasting their time online chatting and playing games. They also told us that the Net has become a point of contention in their households, drawing their kids away from their supervision and into a world that is closed to them. (www.media-awareness.ca/english/research/YCWW/ phaseII/, p. 4)

The Media Awareness Network (2005) goes on to provide profiles of the use of technology for different age groups of young people. Those who are in grades 10 and 11 were found to be using technology 'seamlessly' for a range of both social and academic aspects of their daily lives. Perhaps the most stunning discovery is that 84 per cent of these young people are using instant text-messaging each day for an average of 69 minutes.

These figures alone make clear the extent of contemporary youth participation in modern technologies. But what are young people actually doing and how are they being influenced when they participate in these types of technology? On any given day in Canada, national and local print media, such as *The Globe and Mail,* run first-page journalistic accounts of stories relating to the prevalence of 'cyber-bullying', 'Twitter dangers', and 'cellphone subterfuge' (the methods young people use to text-message in class by circumventing the blockage of satellite systems established by school administrators). To explore these questions we begin by providing a brief but dreadfully neglected history of the rise of the current technological context and two common interpretations of the influence of technology in the lives of young people. It is not sufficient simply to state that young people are highly involved in the technological imperative without discussing how and why they have come to live their lives this way, or without examining the influences they feel in their leisure and work lives. We then offer a critical assessment of these interpretations in light of the further data we present.

A Modern Context for Work and Play

If we trace the origins of the technological context of youth, we find that modern technology originally emerged out of the expansion of the natural sciences as they occurred in the sixteenth and seventeenth centuries (Voegelin, 1948). That expansion resulted from the convergence of a number of complex historical forces, which are only summarized here. Two important changes in attitude and practice stand out for comment. The first change was a growing sense on the part of scientifically minded intellectuals that the world possessed no natural order but was better understood as neutral matter in motion (Cooper, 1991). The second change was a consequence of the first. If the world has no natural order, then it cannot be known through the traditional practices of contemplation and reflection, but must instead be produced through the application of technological procedures that aim to give it a form it lacks by nature (Cooper, 1991). Effectively, this means that we can know only what we make and that nature in the traditional sense is unknowable because it is non-existent.

Cars, computers, and televisions are all things we can know because they have a form that we have given to them. In a sense, modern science justifies experiments restrained by no limits save those of the possible. For instance, nature permits the splitting of atoms; therefore, splitting atoms is seen to be natural. According to this kind of technological imperative, it does not matter that splitting an atom will cause destruction to the world and to human life. We *can* split atoms; therefore we may do so without concerning ourselves with the objection that we have violated nature's order. According to this view, natural is whatever can be done. The political and environmental consequences of these practices are immediately apparent to anyone who wishes to consider the character of twentieth-century totalitarianism and the landscapes of our modern industrial centres.

It is from these ideas that our modern technological world arose. The modern project is an attempt to change the world through technology. (For a more critical assessment see Albert Camus, *The Rebel*, trans. Anthony Bower, New York: Vintage Books, 1991, 188–245.) Though almost always couched in the language of humanitarianism and progress, that ambition has a darker side. The political violence and environmental damage of the early twentieth century were the direct consequences of the same technological revolution that we so actively pursue today. Were these consequences merely temporary glitches in an otherwise sound project? Or were they (and are they still) the inevitable outcome of modernity's utopian ambitions?

The term *utopia* is an important concept in understanding modern society. It is comprised of two Greek words—όυ and τόπρος—which mean, literally, 'no place'. In our contemporary context the word has changed meanings and is now most often associated with the establishment of a perfect regime or society (Cooper, 1991: 203–23). Utopia and technology, therefore, go hand-in-hand, and they are also closely related to another modern political phenomenon— totalitarianism. Technology aspires to a utopian or perfect society. Such a society is perfect precisely because it is total. By *total* we mean that it claims to account for and satisfy all human needs completely. Thus, the modern world strives for a totally technological and perfect existence.

This utopian aspiration toward totality has been vividly portrayed and critically assessed by several contemporary authors. Aldous Huxley's *Brave New World* and George Orwell's *Nineteen Eighty-Four* are good examples of such critical and descriptive work. *Nineteen Eight-Four* in particular stands out as a compelling reminder that our modern pursuit of technological and political perfection comes at a high price. According to Orwell, we cannot inhabit a world devoted to technological perfection and efficiency without sacrificing certain fundamental aspects of our humanity: our ability to love, to show genuine compassion, and even to experience the wonder of human intelligence. Although modern young people live in a world dominated by precisely these technological ambitions, it is remarkable to note how compelling they find analyses such as Orwell's. It is as if his work speaks to a desire long since repressed and their society and gives it voice.

Two general lines of interpretation regarding the utopian character of modern technology have emerged over the past 50 years. The first type of interpretation is apparent in the work of Marshall McLuhan, particularly in his groundbreaking studies of the nature of modern media. McLuhan was a professor of English at the University of Toronto in Canada and later became one of the leading figures in the analysis of modern technology. A second, and opposing, type of interpretation can be found in the work of the French philosopher and social critic Jean Baudrillard, whose books analyze the more modern technological world as young people now experience it.

Marshall McLuhan: The Medium Is Still Really the Message for Young People

McLuhan recognized that the interpretation of technology common in the mid-twentieth century did not adequately describe either its character or the extent of its influence. According to that interpretation, modern technology was no different than early primitive technologies. It was merely a tool that human beings use to accomplish circumscribed and predetermined tasks but that leaves their perceptions of reality entirely unaffected (McLuhan, 1994). (In *Understanding Media*, McLuhan offers the following remarks by a General Sarnoff to describe the view: 'We are too prone to make technological instruments the scapegoats for the sins of those who wield them. The products of modern science are not in themselves good or bad; it is the way they are used that determines their value' (McLuhan, 1994: 11).

McLuhan claims that such a view is inadequate because it fails to appreciate the extent to which technology alters or mediates how we experience ourselves and the world around us. It is the focus on an understanding of experience and *being* with technology that is of value for McLuhan. This is one meaning of his famous phrase 'the medium is the message' (McLuhan, 1994: 7). For instance, the message of television is not in its content or programming but in the act of television watching itself. The same is true of computer technology and even of electric light, the latter of which McLuhan describes as 'pure information' (McLuhan, 1994: 9). These media alter the spatial and temporal ways in which we experience the world: 'The effects of technology do not occur at the level of opinions or concepts, but alter sense ratios or patterns of perception steadily and without any resistance' (McLuhan, 1994: 18).

Recent technological developments seem to confirm McLuhan's thesis. The speed with which information travels and communication occurs has now come close to abolishing the distances in our experiences of space and time. As a result of that near abolition, we experience something close to simultaneity or a kind of non-stop multitasking that we see in the lives of young people who are simultaneously plugged into multiple forms of media each day. One contemporary name for that experience is the ambition to live in 'real time'. This ambition goes a long way to explain our current fascination with 'reality' television, YouTube, and instant text messaging. A break or pause in the constant flow of communication is now experienced by young people almost as a loss of reality. Youth are so completely immersed in a technological world that a technologically unmediated experience of reality seems either false or unreal to them.

Although highly perceptive, McLuhan's analyses were less critical of the range of negative effects of modern technology. For example, he considered technology to be inherently democratic because it de-centralizes power and undermines the controlling forms of earlier mechanical technologies. We can illuminate McLuhan's claim by comparing the oppressive discipline required by early industrial societies with the apparently free and subversive activities made possible by social networking media like Twitter, Facebook, and MSN. Yet McLuhan also recognized that modern technology is totalizing in a way that primitive and mechanical technologies were not. Digital technology creates a 'global village' that, as the term suggests, overcomes the limitations of space and time that are inherent in all older, mechanical technologies. McLuhan attempts to avoid the contradiction by maintaining that the totality made possible by technology is not only valuable for human life but perhaps also a way toward salvation. He claims in this regard that technology's pervasiveness makes possible a human unity that was not previously attainable:

> If the work of the city is the remaking or translating of man into a
> more suitable form than his nomadic ancestors achieved, then might
> not our current translation of our entire lives into the spiritual form of
> information seem to make of the entire globe, and of the human family,
> a single consciousness? (McLuhan, 1994: 61)

McLuhan's 'single consciousness' suggests that by drawing together all human beings into an endless and seamless web of communication, technology promises to eliminate the sources of discord that were in large part the engine of all previous history. For McLuhan this even includes war:

> With the extension of the central nervous system by electric technology,
> even weaponry makes vivid the fact of the unity of the human family.
> The very inclusiveness of information as a weapon becomes a daily
> reminder that politics and history must be recast in the form of 'the
> concretization of human fraternity'. (McLuhan, 1994: 354)

According to McLuhan, technology alters our experiences of the world by being total, simultaneous, and continuous. However, technology also makes possible the achievement of a kind of social harmony or communication in which nature is overcome or perfected. McLuhan's analysis is utopian in this regard. It is also dialectical in it assumptions that a particular object-ive, if pursued to its final term, will produce its antithesis. This is the assumption that lies behind McLuhan's assertion that the active pursuit of technological weaponry (war) will result in the production of 'human fraternity' (peace).

Jean Baudrillard: Youth's State of Constant Electrocution

Jean Baudrillard's first major studies of modern technology appeared roughly 30 years after the publication of McLuhan's *Understanding Media*—beginning with *The Transparency of Evil*, which appeared in 1990. The most relevant works that followed it are *The Gulf War Did Not Take Place* (1995), *The Perfect Crime* (1996), *Screened Out* (2002), and *The Spirit of Terrorism* (2002). From this historical vantage point, Baudrillard was able to observe the shapes that technology had assumed in the years following McLuhan's work. Though nodding occasionally to McLuhan's accomplishments, Baudrillard is far less sanguine about the character and consequences of the technological enterprise than was McLuhan. Baudrillard offers a critical analysis of both the dialectical and utopian aspirations of modern technology.

Baudrillard describes the modern aspiration toward perfection negatively. He also criticizes the idea that communication can be complete and the total flow of information nonstop and transparent, although both are central demands of modern digital technology. For communication to be both efficient and continuous nothing can be hidden; all must be plain. However, for Baudrillard this attempt to achieve complete transparency and simultaneity also has its price—paradoxically it requires the elimination of content or meaning from the act of communication itself:

> In order for content to be conveyed as well and as quickly as possible,
> that content should come as close as possible to transparency and
> insignificance. This principle may be seen in action in telephone
> relationships or in media transmissions—as also in more serious arenas.
> Thus *good* communication—the foundation, today, of a *good* society—
> implies the annihilation of its own content. (Baudrillard, 1993: 49)

In order for communication to be fast (both fundamental demands of technology) it must be virtually without substance or content. That is why 24-hour television news offers so little analysis of the events it describes. What matters is not the event itself or even that it is fully 'known' but rather that there is nonstop communication about it. As Baudrillard writes, '[what] if information referred not to events but to the promotion of information itself *qua* event? If communication were concerned not with messages but instead with the promotion of communication itself *qua* myth?' (Baudrillard, 1993: 50).

This is the imperative of modern technological communication and it applies equally well to modern human life and experience. According to Baudrillard the loss of reality in the world around us is matched by a corresponding loss of reality in ourselves. The person who is most transparent is the one most lacking in substance or character. Technological communication requires guaranteed conviviality (as our contemporary form of offering welcome is no longer 'don't mention it' but 'no worries'). Conviviality requires the removal of character because character is an inevitable source of conflict in a world in which there are many who are unwilling to follow its imperfect promptings. Technology aims to remove such conflicts by rendering all decisions of principle and meaning a matter of indifference. Thus, technology moves toward its complete realization silences principled debates and diminishes genuine human encounters. In the more direct language of *The Perfect Crime*, Baudrillard argues that, far from perfecting reality, modern technology is responsible for its murder (Baudrillard, 1996: 1–7). The virtual reality created by our technologies is not reality but a strategy for escaping it and selling its facsimile back to young people on the open market.

This escape is motivated both by a weakening of our resolve to face life's harshest aspects and a desire to master things beyond our control. And there is always the market incentive to sell products to cover the flaws in the procedure. Contemporary youth culture's obsession with the newest technological gadgets is clearly something in which capital is implicated and from which it makes a tidy profit. The Canadian Council on Learning (2009) reports that last year sales in the American video game industry quadrupled from 1996, reaching 11.7 billion in 2008. Yet according to McLuhan and Baudrillard, in the creation of these technologies there is an even more serious matter at stake than capitalist exploitation, although capitalist exploitation itself may be symptomatic of that issue.

The Drive to Totality and Cyborgian Existence

The world of young people is filled with a host of material artifacts of culture. These artifacts range from blue jeans to cars, from MP3 players to radio stations, from books to televisions. All artifacts shape the lives of young people in some measure. This is a characteristic common to all forms of technology, both ancient and modern. Anything that engages young people's attention has this effect; it mediates their experience of reality. However, with the advent of modern technology this ambition has moved beyond any traditional attempt to mediate or ameliorate the human condition. As mentioned earlier, for McLuhan and Baudrillard, modern technology's aim is totality. If we examine this ambition in relation to modern screen technologies, its totalizing character will become clear.

Modern screen technology is ubiquitous in contemporary Western societies. There is virtually no physical place and no intellectual or emotional aspect of human experience that has not been co-opted by a screen. In the case of young people this means that everything they experience is mediated by this technological device. The current drive toward portability and personal biotechnologies does not mark a new stage in technological development but rather merely the working out of technology's original ambitions. As this totality becomes more seamless, direct contact with unmediated reality becomes rare. It does not matter that young people occasionally 'tune out' or 'unplug' or enjoy a little 'downtime'. Once technology achieves this level of saturation it is no longer merely 'out there' as an external artifact. Rather, it has become part of the very way in which young people see and experience life. This leads us to the following question: What is the young person's experience of life, and what does this mean for her freedom, education, leisure, and work?

The consequence of this drive to totality is that technology has insinuated itself into every relationship young people have with other human beings and with the world. When the screen becomes total, it no longer 'mediates' reality—it replaces it. The fetishlike character of young people's participation in modern technology has its explanation here. Youth hold on to these devices, and their digital images, with such tenacity because they are the only reality youth have left. And, as Latham (2002), following Marx, attests, young people then fetishize the commodity by making the thing itself the real object of desire. They desire it at all costs and ignore the processes by which it came into being. Those deprived of technology or with outdated machines are excluded from company as a matter of principle. They are cut off from 'reality', as it were, and therefore are almost unreal.

Nonetheless, what exists on the screen is not yet what exists in the world itself. The screen offers only the appearance of reality, not its substance or meaning. Young people who have been raised on these devices (and there is now in existence an entire generation for which this is true) are product- and image-savvy but limited in their understanding of what these images mean or conceal. There is a strong need for media literacy, political analytical ability, and resistance. These ideas will be reviewed again in Chapter 8. For now, we move this discussion of the modern technological context into the everyday lives of youth leisure and labour, or, rather, of youth at work and at play.

Box 5.1 Youth Commodities

At the full end of the spectrum of commodity fetishism in the lives of youth are the situations in which a commodity is exchanged for life itself. A host of stories in print media, such as the *Ottawa Citizen* and *The Globe and Mail*, have recently reported injuries and deaths of young people for items such as MP3 players. Indeed, a black market of youth commodities can be found in many urban communities and appears to be growing. When you search the Internet for such stories, what do you find? What are the trends and experiences for young people as reported by journalists? Is this a true problem or a demonized representation of the culture of youth?

Youth at Play

Baudrillard's and McLuhan's analyses of modern technology provide us with a good place to rejoin the discussion of modern young people and the effects of technology on their lives and leisure pursuits. It is also the place where we can reach some conclusion about the value of these respective interpretations of modern technology. In *Grown Up Digital* (Tapscott, 2009), it is suggested that the generation of young people who have been born into this technological explosion are the 'Net Generation' and are demonstrating an ongoing, total, and seamless use of multiple technologies. This is corroborated in a 2010 report on young people and media use wherein music accounts for 2.31 hours per day, TV and all its content for 4.29 hours per day, computer screens for 1.29 hours per day, and video games for 1.13 hours per day for a total of 10.45 hours per day of media exposure (Kaiser Foundation, 2010). In addition, the video gaming media entertainment young people are so engrossed in is modelled after the very technologies that are used in modern war and work (Dyer-Witheford, 2003).

Young people stare at screens while at school, they use screens while at work, and they stare at screens while at home. And when they leave school, work, and home behind, they distract themselves in public by watching screens on which are depicted the lives of people whose home life and labour and education are taken up essentially with staring at screens. Technology is a narcotic, according to one of McLuhan's more critical formulations (McLuhan, 1994, 41–ff), and young people today are hooked. Screens are that narcotic's most powerful and pervasive form, and they are becoming more so by the day. The contemporary purveyors of technology have ensured that our young people have a constant and ready supply. There is no private space that has not been co-opted by a screen; and there is almost no public space that has not been privatized in the same way. Even a ride on a bus with young people through rural Canadian communities demonstrates the totalized and simultaneous cyborgian nature of this generation's use of technology. Each one is plugged into an MP3 player's pervasive music, using either their own player or sharing headphones with a friend. Each carries a phone and sends multiple text messages, and no two are engaged in more than limited conversation, most of which concerns the newest music or product. Their speech sounds like a televised version of itself, and could just as easily be coming from the mouth of a youth in New York:

> Almost all (94 percent) of the top 50 sites include marketing material.
> Although advertising is ubiquitous, marketing messages are also
> often embedded in content. For example, every game on the popular
> site Candystand incorporates images of various Lifesaver products.
> Neopets' virtual village, Neopia Central, has a Disney Theatre where
> kids can watch Disney movie clips or play games based on popular
> Disney movie characters. The prevalence of these types of marketing

practices is particularly noteworthy because over three-quarters of
kids who play product-centred games think that these games are not
'mainly advertisements' but 'just games'. Awareness of the commercial
nature of these games rises with age (from 19 percent of kids in Grade
4 to 31 percent of kids in Grade 11), but the large majority of kids do
not critically question the presence of branded products in their virtual
playgrounds. (Media Awareness Network, 2005)

The deeper concern posed by technological society is that these visual
images have the appearance of reality but little or none of its content. That is
in large measure their charm and their appeal. However, this lack of content
and context is also the reason why Baudrillard (1996: 1–7) claims visual
technologies have brought about 'the murder of reality'. Less hyperbolically,
we might say they have 'eclipsed' reality. The consequence of this change is
not merely that students' school grades have dropped and that students report
lower levels of personal contentment (Kaiser Foundation, 2010). (For an
analysis of this phenomenon of contemporary illiteracy in the German context,
see Eric Voegelin, 'The German University and the Order of German Society:
A Reconsideration of the Nazi Era' in *Collected Works: Published Essays 1966–
1985*, Vol. 12, Baton Rouge: Louisiana State University Press, 1990, 1–35.) The
real problem is a loss of reality or substance in life that issues in a corresponding
loss of reality or substance in us. The nature and extent of that loss begins to
reveal itself as we examine more closely the lives of modern young people.

While it may be true that young people claim to find the use of technology
'compelling and important', they are grappling with technology at precisely the
same time they are struggling for autonomy, status, friendship, self-expression,
and identity (Ito et al., 2008). Ito and her team have recently published the
Digital Youth Project from over 800 interviews with youth, parents, and
educators. They also conducted over 5,000 hours of online observations as part
of the most extensive US study of youth media use. (The book arising from
the study is *Hanging Out, Messing Around, and Geeking Out: Kids Living and
Learning with New Media*, Cambridge, MA: MIT Press, 2009.) While the data
are rich in descriptions about the form and use of technology, the study suggests
a cheerleading about what is essentially technology's pervasive vampirism,
reminiscent of McLuhan. The absence of a critical analysis is surprising given
their findings that young people were 'always on' and attempting to maintain
'a continuous presence, or co-presence, in multiple contexts' (Ito et al., 2008).
The *Digital Youth Project Report* shows the ubiquity of technology in the
everyday worlds of young people at home, school, community, and work. But
no discussion of the outcome of such experience is attempted. What does it
mean to young people to be forever plugged in to screens?

Critical answers would confirm Baudrillard's claim that our constant
participation in modern technology is like being in 'a state of permanent

electrocution' (Baudrillard, 1993: 32). Indeed, a study of school cultures in Canada evidenced student complaints about media such as Facebook's 'honesty box' as the next level of ongoing 'meanness' from which they cannot escape at the day's end (Tilleczek et al., 2008). The Canadian Council on Social Development (2006) sites a Media Awareness Network study (2001) showing that one-quarter of all young Canadian Internet users had received emails containing hateful messages about others, and a British survey in 2002 found that one-quarter of youth aged 11 to 19 had been harassed via computer or cellphone. As well, a recent US study found that 57 per cent of students in grades 4 to 8 had someone say hurtful or angry things to them online, and 13 per cent said that this happened frequently. The latter study also found that 35 per cent of students had been threatened online and that 42 per cent had been bullied while on the Internet. However, 58 per cent of those surveyed had not informed their parents about these incidents, which suggests a process of normalization of such events. Data from the United Kingdom similarly shows indications of the normalization of violent and narcotic experiences of digital leisure. Furlong & Cartmel (2007) report that the computer gaming industry rivals the music industry with eight million copies of the new release *Grand Theft Auto* sold in eight weeks and *Super Mario*'s total sales reaching 181 million copies. Young people in the United Kingdom who play these games spend an average of 11 hours per week doing so. The United States, however, is ahead in game sales with forecasts of over 250 million units between 1995 and 2009.

The egocentrism of young people generally is due in large part to the intensity and newness of their life experiences coupled with developing cognitive and emotional capacity, meaning-making, and judgments. Important social theorists such as Jean Piaget, Robert Selman, David Elkind, and Irving Goffman have had much to say about these developments, which are too numerous to cover here. As young people age, their experiences acquire greater depth and maturity from repeated encounters with events and things that are no longer completely novel. Essential for this development in young people are meaningful and sustained encounters with realities other than themselves—i.e., with people, places, and things. Yet, it is precisely such encounters that modern screen technologies prevent, although their increasingly high-definition character tends to create the opposite impression. Indeed, Putnam (2000) has demonstrated the loss of civic engagement among young people as a consequence of increasing solitary pursuits over the past 20 years. Modern technological experience has played a significant role in bringing about these changes.

The argument that passivity or detachment has been overcome by the 'interactive' character of modern screen technology is false. It is true that interactive technologies do entail an additional level of active engagement and socializing in comparison to television and movies, but that involvement does not rival an unmediated experience of reality. What one encounters in cyberspace is not the 'other' but an avatar of oneself. Rojeck's (1985) trends for the pursuits of modernity—privatization, individualization, commercialization, and pacification—appear to be gathering steam in youth cultures. As we will see in the following chapter, the social networking and sociability uses of technology are also changing the nature of youth friendships. How individualized, commoditized, and pacified young people are becoming, and the character of their ongoing and expanding forays into the technological project, is a matter of central concern. It remains to be seen how these experiences and technological consumer structures carve up and continue to reproduce patterns of inequality for youth.

Technology is a human construction, not an organically occurring phenomenon. The medium itself is therefore only a reflection of us and merely an occasion for experience. Though it is possible to subordinate any existing thing to a desire for experience alone, screen technologies make this disposition even more likely given the absence of any genuine content or bodily presence. On the screen all that remains of the other is an appearance that stimulates our senses. Meaning or substance, which is the foundation of human relationships, is excluded on principle. And what if we plan to spend our leisure hours this way? Play was once a shared activity with potential for loving relationships and open expression of self. From their perch within these technological nests, young people state that the most 'unhealthy' things they do each week involve staring at too many screens and eating junk food (Tilleczek et al., 2008). Is there a way through this modern looking glass? Too often the research concerned with these matters suggests that we will empower young people by simply teaching them about the negative potential of the content of the materials they see online or about gaining more privacy or about finding authentication of online materials. Young people are better posed to be invited into a true, critical examination of technology's influence on human social experience. We examine youth social actions and movements in Chapter 8 as alternative means by which youth are reacting:

> Technologies like television, VCRs and camcorders suture everyday life
> into a mediated image continuum, and interface with computers—
> whether overt in the form of PC units, or less obvious in the form
> of data banks and other regulative and surveillance systems—is a
> prosthetic connection within the labour and leisure practice of everyone.
> Appropriately enough, it was Baudrillard who has summed up the
> resulting situation, arguing that the contemporary individual seems to
> subsist 'as a terminal of networks . . . endowed with telematic power—
> that is, with the capability of regulating everything from a distance,
> including work, consumption, play, social relations and leisure. As
> interface with such informational networks increasingly comes to define
> the substance of social interaction, contemporary experience becomes an
> ongoing articulation into cyborg possibility. (Latham, 2002: 16)

Youth at Work

Similar to the leisure pursuits of youth, participation in the labour market is affected by complex, modern, social, economic, and political forces. The emerging experience of technology, space, and time has crept into work. Work contexts are conceived of as transient and flexible and so, too, are young people describing their connections to the labour market. The broader and interconnected contexts of youth work are described as including the more complicated and fractured paths between school and work. And the kinds of work that youth are engaged in are shifting. The outcomes are an elongation of the period of youth as a result of longer periods of dependency on their families; shifts in dominant forms of all labour; the use of young people as a source of inexpensive labour in the growing service industry; and the place of youth as consumers. We see trends toward greater and earlier participation by young people in the labour force to fulfill what Baudrillard terms insatiable 'consummativity' (1981:83). One small but obvious place to witness the tensions in these forces is the ongoing debate around shifting minimum wage for youth workers. In Canada the hourly minimum youth wages are highest in Alberta, and Ontario's provincial Liberal government is currently in the throes of controversy relating to their clawback in the promised increase of minimum wages. The interests of industry, education, politicians, and young people are heard in these competing directions.

Modern Labour Market Contexts

Furlong and Cartmel (2007) have this to say about the youth labour market:

> The restructuring of the adult labour market and the decline of the youth labour market have important implications for the way young people experience the transition to work on a subjective level. These changes, which stem from the continued decline in demand for low-skill labour, have led to a demand for better educated, more skilled labour force in advanced industrial societies. But the speed of change has meant that the current generation of young people are making their transition to work in a period of turmoil (which is perhaps a characteristic of modern labour markets) and, as a consequence, may lack clear frames of reference which can help smooth transitions. (Furlong & Carmel, 2007: 50)

Furlong and Cartmel go on to argue that it is more difficult for young people to secure work without an education while, conversely, it appears that there is a stable and predictable job market in which their parents, many of whom did not pursue post-secondary education, have been employed. Young people are therefore negotiating and regulating these contexts. In Canada, as in most industrialized countries, more young people are staying in school for longer periods of time. When young people finish their schooling and seek work, they enter a difficult labour market that offers them mainly part-time, temporary, or contract positions. Of the 1.1 million Canadian young people aged 15 to 24 working part-time in 2004, 20 per cent said they did so because of labour market conditions and because they could not find full-time jobs. Indeed, one of every three unemployed workers in Canada today is a young person (Canadian Council on Social Development, 2006). Their unemployment rate declined from 18 per cent in 1994 to 13 per cent in 2004. But it is still higher than in 1989 (11 per cent). This youth unemployment rate is more than double that of adults aged 25 to 44 (6.5 per cent) (CCSD, 2006). But young people with post-secondary education are much less likely to be unemployed (8 per cent of youth with a university degree) compared to youth with less than high school, statistics which only serve to reinforce how the youth labour market continues to reproduce social class positions.

Not surprisingly, the youth labour market also reproduces cultural inequalities for youth even while it seems flexible and open. According to a recent study by the Canadian Labour Congress (cited in CCSD, 2006), Aboriginal and visible minority youth have higher unemployment rates than their Caucasian counterparts. In 2001, the unemployment rate for Aboriginal youth aged 15 to 24 was 23 per cent, compared to 14 per cent for all youth. According to the CLC study, visible minority youth—and black youth, in particular—have lower employment rates than the average. Forty-one per cent of visible minority youth were born in Canada, which means they were almost certainly educated in the Canadian system and speak English or French well. Yet in 2001, only 44 per cent of all visible minority youth aged 15 to 24 and 48 per cent of those born in Canada were employed, compared to 58 per cent of all youth. And among black youth born in Canada, only 33 per cent were employed. It remains to be seen if modern Canadian working class and visible minority youth are, as Willis argued in the 1970s, getting 'working class jobs' due to their process of foreclosure on schooling and selection of working class jobs. There have been few examinations of the social reproduction of inequalities inherent in the new youth labour market:

> Paul Willis explained the experiences of lower working class boys in
> terms of their resistance to middle class school cultures which were seen
> as largely irrelevant to their future lives in manual occupations. Today
> the cultural dimensions of decisions about educational participation
> are recognised as being more complex and tending not to involve such
> strong cultural-based rejections of the value and benefits of extended
> education. The increased emphasis placed on educational attainment in
> virtually all social groups stems, in part, from a growing awareness of the

importance of credentials in the modern economy. It can also be linked
to a breakdown of a visible dichotomy in the labour market between
working class and middle class jobs that has accompanied the decline
of manufacturing industry, a more educated parentage and a greater
emphasis on equal opportunities. (Furlong, 2008: 2)

The increased participation of the majority of young people in the labour
market is a point of discussion. Young people living in the 1990s were twice as
likely to be employed as those living in the 1950s (Kusum, 1998). The US has
the highest percentage of young people in the workforce of any other Western
nation with 3.7 million (aged 15 to 17) employed (Layne et al., 1994; Moskowitz,
2004). In Canada over the past decade, a higher proportion of young people
aged 15 to 24 have also been participating in the labour force (either working
or looking for work) with 68 per cent in 2004, compared to 64 per cent in 1994
(CCSD, 2006). However, actual working participation rates are lower than the
pre-recession rates of 1989. By comparison, the employment rate for Canadian
adults aged 25 to 44 rose over that same period, from 79 per cent in 1989 to
82 per cent by 2004 (CCSD, 2006). According to the Canadian Labour Force
Survey (Statistics Canada, 2003), young workers between the ages of 15 and 24
represent about 15 per cent of the Canadian workforce. Sixty-nine per cent of
young people between the ages of 15 and 19, and 89 per cent of young people
between the ages of 20 and 24 reported that they had been employed during
that past year. Given these social, economic, and technological contexts of the
youth labour market, what are the experiences of work for young people?

Life at Work

Young people often begin their experience in the paid workforce early (Frone,
1998) with as many as 40 per cent of students in the seventh and eighth
grades and 47 per cent of high school students between the ages of 16 and 18
employed during the school year (Manning, 1990). Bachman and Schulenberg
(1993) show 75 per cent of high school students employed during the school
year and 46 per cent of these students working in excess of 20 hours per week.
Krahn (1991) found similar trends in Canada, with 54 per cent of full-time
students between the ages of 15 and 19 years participating in the labour force.
The Canadian Council on Social Development (CCSD) (2006) reports that
employment trends for teens aged 15 to 19 are similar to those of young people
aged 15 to 24. Employed teens as a proportion of their peers remained virtually
unchanged from 2002 to 2004, at 45 per cent. Not surprisingly, the CCSD also
reports a difference in employment rates depending on the region, with the
highest rate in Alberta; the lowest was in Newfoundland in 2004.

What do these school-aged youth do at work? The National Longitudinal
Survey of Children and Youth (NLSCY) data is reported by the CCSD (2006) to

show that in Canada more than one in five (22 per cent) youth aged 14 and 15 in 2000 worked for an employer in the previous week, up from 16 per cent in 1998. Forty-eight per cent said they had worked for pay at odd jobs (up from 36 per cent in 1998), 14 per cent had worked at a family business, and 18 per cent had worked without pay. When asked what kind of job they had worked at most in the previous week, odd jobs came out on top, at 52 per cent. Nine per cent had worked in a restaurant, 8 per cent in a store, and 6 per cent in other service jobs. The majority of young working teens (70 per cent) work fewer than 10 hours per week, down from 73 per cent in 1998.

Young men and women worked virtually the same number of hours per week, but youth in low-income families worked more—33 per cent aged 14 and 15 in low-income families (under $40,000) worked more than 10 hours a week, compared with 28 per cent of those in higher-income families. More than three-quarters (78 per cent) of young teens said they had worked during the summer, up from 62 per cent in 1998. One-quarter had worked for pay for an employer, and almost two-thirds had done odd jobs.

In 2004, young people in Canada (aged 15 to 24) earned an average of $10.49 per hour. In constant dollars, that was up only slightly (1.7 per cent) from 1997. The average hourly wage of youth is 56.7 per cent that of all workers. In 2003, youth aged 15 to 24 earned an average of $8,900 per year at work. Taking income from all sources into account, their average income that year was $10,200. Teenagers (aged 15 to 19) earned much less, with average yearly earnings in 2003 at $4,200, compared to $12,700 for young adults (aged 20 to 24) (CCSD, 2006). When youth seek work it is often part-time to offset post-secondary tuition and living expenses, and many still receive money from their parents. More than three-quarters (77 per cent) of youth aged 14 and 15 received money from their parents in the previous week, with 70 per cent receiving $40 or less (CCSD, 2006).

A review of literature relating to the experiences and outcomes of youth work found evidence that work has the potential to teach responsibility, punctuality, skills in interacting with the public, and managing finances. In addition, young people seem to concede to the personal benefits of work, including valuable work experience, cultural exposure, opportunities for socialization, a degree of financial independence, acquisition of new skills, and an opportunity to explore career goals (Blanco et al., 2005). Other studies have indicated that increased part-time employment can have a positive effect on future employment outcomes (Carr et al., 1996), and part-time employment can be beneficial when young people themselves view their jobs as providing them with skills that will be useful in the future (Mortimer et al., 1991).

However, too much work or the wrong kind of work can have negative effects for youth. High school students who worked 20 hours or more outside of regular school hours had lower grade point averages than students who worked fewer hours and those who did not have any form of remunerated employment

(Marsh, 1991). Steinberg et al. (1993) has noted a consensus in the literature such that it is not work itself but rather the long hours of employment (i.e., in excess of 20 hours per week) that may be deleterious to youth, a finding substantiated by Cheng (1995). Indeed, it is conceivable that poverty and the *need to work* are behind many problematic outcomes for young people (Newman, 1999). The reasons for work range across social class lines from the desire for additional spending money to the necessity of feeding families.

It is no surprise that young workers tend to hold a disproportionate number of unattractive jobs. Young people find their paid work primarily in the lower level service industries, such as retail sales, food and beverage services, and janitorial work. In general, these types of jobs offer part-time hours and require few skills. These types of lower level jobs are also by nature very transitory. As such, Loughlin and Barling (1999) note that much of the research into youth employment has traditionally focused on the effects of the quantity of work rather than the quality of work. But with many entry-level positions now becoming permanent employment for young people (Krahn, 1991) this trend has incited examination of the quality of youth work. It is here that we rejoin our discussion of technology and its influences on the working lives of youth.

The 'McJobs' of the service industry are most often subject to intense routinization, speed, close surveillance, and management control, yet at the same time they also demand high levels of self-motivation and investment from workers in highly stressful conditions. Tannock (2001) listed several factors that young people correlated to their workplace, including difficult relations with managers and customers (being treated poorly), repetitive work tasks, low occupational status, low wages, continual workplace surveillance, as well as hot, greasy, and often dangerous work environments. The primary cause of problems, however, was the lack of time in which to complete required work duties, a finding that repeats itself in examinations of youth work cultures. The sense of powerlessness pervades and while it is established by the myriad structures of the jobs, the young people drift home feeling personally 'responsible' and defeated, the fast-food chain's customer relations' 'ten commandments' ringing in their ears: 'The customer does us an honor when he calls; we are not doing him a favor by serving him', and 'The customer is not someone to argue with or match wits with . . .' (Leidner, 2003). Just as the culture of youth driving has been overlooked as a response to traffic injuries and fatalities (Tilleczek, 2006) so, too, has the culture of youth work been obscured in research about individualizes the issues. Further examination is required of youth work for its technological and structural barriers to confident and meaningful participation in society.

And finally, what are young people doing with the money they acquire at work? This brings us full circle to the introduction and context of the chapter. Modern technology and its consumption are bound up in both play and work—leisure and labour processes. Modern technology has insinuated itself into the range of cultural nests for youth and become an integral part of the complex process and outcomes of the everyday lives of youth. It is now more difficult than ever to experience divisions between work and leisure; both are technologically driven and maintained by consumerism. At the risk of being further marginalized and isolated, young people are running to keep up with the project while slowly losing connections. They are also losing the potential for meaningful and political participation in societal discussions. Indeed, we argue that youth and youth studies provide a critical pulse for the manners in which the modern project is moving forward.

One critical place to start is to provide a space in youth studies for young people to discuss, critique, and understand the modern project and its technological/consumptive reach. Too many studies simply outline and itemize the extent to which technologies are used and/or provide a whitewash of its influences. A more balanced and full portrayal of the daily life of youth at work and play is required.

Critical Thinking Activities

1. Return to your notes on mapping out the passages between child and youth from Chapter 1. What were all of the rites of passage you mapped out for yourself? Where do technology, work, leisure, and the media fit in to your life transitions?

2. Watch the remaining segments of the *Merchants of Cool* (see Suggested Websites, p. 86) that describe the process that corporations and marketers are using to sell 'cool' back to young people. What does this mean for the lives of young people? Link the documentary film to the ideas presented in this chapter on 'consummativity' and 'consuming youth'.

3. How would you begin to research the negative effects of technology on the daily lives of young people? Map out a brief methodology and method based on what you have learned in Chapters 3, 4, and 5.

Further Readings

Dyer-Witheford, N., de Peuter , G., & Kline, S. (2003). *Digital Play: The Interaction of Technology, Culture, and Marketing*. Montreal: McGill-Queen's University Press.

Latham, R. (2002a). The cybernetic vampire of consumer youth culture. In *Consuming Youth: Vampires, Cyborgs and the Culture of Consumption* (pp. 1–25). Chicago: University of Chicago Press.

————. (2002b). Fast sofas and cyborg couch potatoes: Generation X on the Infobahn. In *Consuming Youth: Vampires, Cyborgs and the Culture of Consumption* (pp. 180–215). Chicago: University of Chicago Press.

Willets, D. (2010). *The Pinch: How the Baby Boomers Took Their Children's Future—And Why They Should Give It Back*. United Kingdom: Atlantic Books.

Suggested Websites

The Globe and Mail: 'So you thought Generation X was angry?' www.theglobeandmail.com/life/style/so-you-thought-generation-x-was-angry/article1457660/

Merchants of Cool www.pbs.org/wgbh/pages/frontline/shows/cool/view/

Chapter Six

Schools, Families, and Friends: Tangled Social Webs

It is astonishing how little systematic study is devoted to the institutional 'anthropology' of schooling given its situatedness and its exposure to the changing social and economic climate. Its relation to the family, to the economy, to religious institutions, even to the labour market, is only vaguely understood.... (Bruner, 1996; 34–35)

Almost everyone has had the occasion to look back upon his school days and wonder what has become of the knowledge he was supposed to have amassed during his years of schooling, and why it is that the technical skills he acquired have to be learned over again in changed form in order to stand him in good stead. Indeed, he is lucky who does not find that in order to make progress, in order to go ahead intellectually, he does not have to unlearn much of what he learned in school. The questions cannot be disposed of by saying that the subjects were not actually learned, for they were learned at least sufficiently to enable a pupil to pass examinations in them. One trouble is that the subject-matter in question was learned in isolation; it was put, as it were, in a water-tight compartment . . . and hence is so disconnected from the rest of experience that it is not available under the actual conditions of life. (Dewey, 1938: 47–48)

Introduction

Schools are important places for young people and critical sites for youth studies. Indeed, the 'schooled child' is an entrenched social norm that arose in the last quarter of the nineteenth century (Hendrick, 2001) and the modern 'schooled society' (Davies & Guppy, 2006) is one in which formal education occupies an ever-present cultural centre. Schools, and the school experience, exert a strong influence on contemporary young people since they spend a good deal of time in classrooms with their same-age peers, being 'trained' or educated for their future in rapidly shifting labour markets. Both age segregation and the ongoing centrality of education have a profound impact on youth work, leisure, friendships, and families. Understanding youth requires examination of a host of in-school and out-of-school experiences and influences that cross institutional barriers and delineate the daily lives of young people.

This chapter picks up where Chapter 5 left off in this examination. It further describes and discusses the legacies of the modern and technological society on schools, families, and friends. These outcomes, and their impacts on youth and the future of education, are a serious, yawning issue in youth studies. This chapter begins with a discussion of education and school by examining the debates around the purposes and structures of schools, what is taught, by whom, and how. The question of who gets to decide on the character of contemporary education is also posed. Critical questions about the aims of school are less often considered in youth studies in comparison to the technical aspects of curriculum and teaching that take centre stage in research. But school structures, strategies, and techniques require grounding in the purposes and influences of education for contemporary youth, including a thorough understanding of the changing character of social institutions outside of the school.

However, there are emerging signals of schools isolating themselves from the complex cultural nests of youth. They have distanced themselves from families and other community agencies that may assist young people. This is a trend to watch since schools cannot act alone in invoking the well-being of young people and there are some current efforts to reach out to families and communities. Still, a good deal of practice in schools suggests that schools act as if they alone *can* 'educate' youth. This chapter of the book therefore seeks to identify the differences between *education* and *school* as young people see them. It places schools and education within the complex cultural nests of communities, families, and friends, and builds on the stage set in Chapter 5 vis-à-vis technological, media, and consumer influences. Such influences do not disappear at the school boundary, and market forces also permeate daily learning spaces.

The social organization of these influences can highlight how the reproduction of social inequalities and/or stages for resistance are set. The life stories and biographies of youth are written on these social stages. These biographical and narrative identity processes, and the fundamental place of *being* and experience, are the focus of Chapter 7. The current chapter connects to the importance of biographical process by reconsidering the fundamental social processes of *being, becoming,* and *belonging* as integral to education, friendships, and family life.

Redressing Education and Schools for Youth

Our analysis of the aims and functions of education and schools begins with a discussion of the character of contemporary education and with the selection of three of many approaches to understanding education. Each approach follows from the discussion in Chapter 5 of the wider society as fundamentally technological in orientation. Within this social context have emerged competing and contested ideas and practices about education. I argue that education and the processes of schooling are fundamentally about the treatment and lives of young people, since education's centrality in contemporary society sets an agenda for their lives. However, not all discussions about education acknowledge or include this centrality or the needs of youth. Instead, many theories concentrate on the nebulous desires of the technological society.

Three Approaches to the Character of Contemporary Education

Education for Technicians and Technological Education

The first set of ideas about education that have been posited is that our various educational institutions should seek to match society's technological and modern character. In this view, education is largely a matter of preparing individual young people for life in a technological society. This preparation includes both the acquisition of the technical training necessary for gainful employment and the cultivation of the intellectual habits that are necessary for participation in a wider range of social activities. In the US and Canadian contexts, the benefits of such technology-driven education have not been obvious. Concerns are frequently expressed in educational literature about declining levels of literacy among modern young people, particularly their ability to read (Willms, 1999) and do mathematics (Case, Griffen, & Kelly, 1999). The claim that technology heightens or enhances our grasp of reality is compromised by these and other findings. There is a curious irony that constant participation in modern screen technologies seems to diminish the very skills necessary to create and continue the technological project itself. But as Srigley (forthcoming) asserts, there are more troubling aspects of technology's ambition than this ironic self-destruction such that technological relevance becomes primary to all other goals. Any approach that addresses the question of education and the cultivation of young people's capacities in any other way is considered antiquated and irrelevant. Furthermore, individual achievement and success take precedence in education and schooling practices and are defined by a cadre of standardized measurements. Such tests attempt to measure individual performance and success with an eye always to the acquisition of certain kinds of skills necessary for participation in the technological world. The practices, arts, and content of education may be reduced to a set of techniques to serve this end. Alternative forms of humanities programs and courses do currently exist but they are under fire by the dominant ethos that measures value solely in terms of a subject's immediate usefulness for modern technological life (cf. Nussbaum, 2010).

However, given the extraordinary rate at which technological change now occurs, more poorly funded public sector educational institutions have a good deal of difficulty even achieving comparable levels of technical sophistication to that of industry. Indeed, it is not uncommon to find that the curriculum of many training programs will be technically obsolete by the time students have completed their studies. Moreover, the slow but steady leak of technology and advertising into schools could be precisely counter to the goals of education and freedom as John Dewey so eloquently perceived them in *Education and Experience*. This begs us to consider the following: What are the experiences of screen technologies and modern technological life for young people? What is it like to grow up in a highly commodified culture? Do these experiences interrupt, rupture, or support the goals of education as we see them?

Education for Young People

A second set of ideas relating to contemporary education are critical of the first and attempt to answer the questions posed above. The criticisms are related to the problems in overlooking the evidence we have about young people themselves. These second sets of voices come mainly from developmental and later cultural psychology as they attempted to take context and culture into account. One could follow the Jean Piaget and Lev Vygotsky conversations through this field and fruitfully find the main threads and foci. Their work has inspired thousands of contemporary scholars who study youth and education.

The focus of this set of ideas has been a slow but steady suggestion that the needs and requirements of youth (as arrived at mainly from developmental psychology) must be considered in educational processes. What is the match between what we know about young people and how they can best achieve success in school? What are the contexts within which young people live and learn? Indeed, today the 'positive youth development' and resiliency

---

Box 6.1 Piaget and Vygotsky and Youth Development

A quick Internet search on 'Piaget and Vygotsky' will lead to innumerable essays, debates, and YouTube formulations of their respective theories of youth development. After searching their names, find three sources that best assist you in understanding how each theorist took the social context and/ or culture into account in the consideration of learning and education. After arriving at this general idea of their work, find one primary source of each of their writings and write a two-page synopsis for each. Focus on what their work would mean for educational practice in secondary schools today. How do both Jean Piaget and Lev Vygotsky make the intellectual development of young people visible in educational processes? (CF. Vygotsky, 1929, 1978, 1986; and Piaget, 1958, 1972.)

movements suggest that a pathological model of young people as naturally flawed is not of use in answering these questions. As the brief social history of youth in Chapter 2 suggests, this body of work argues that the strength and potential of young people become a focal point in opposition to the earlier pathological psychological evidence that aimed at finding out what was wrong with (and therefore spending time simply providing labels for) those who did not succeed. In that earlier set of ideas, individual students were seen as the main location of problems and as such there were no serious discussions about the roles and responsibilities of the forms, structures, and goals of education and modern schooling. More will be said about the details of these debates in Chapter 7.

Education *with* and *for* Young People and Society

While partly praiseworthy for putting young people as central in the picture, there is much more that social sciences and humanities can tell us about the lives, times, and forms of education best suited to young people. Alternative ideas and programs of education acknowledge the practical affairs of economic life as legitimate and necessary concerns of a genuinely civil society, but they also reach beyond such matters in order to explore facets of life that are acquired with greater difficulty and are essential to a good life.

Srigley (forthcoming) suggests a further discussion of the components of such a life is found in Iris Murdoch's *The Sovereignty of the Good* (1970). He also cites Cooper (1991) to argue that these facets of life range from the nature of friendship to the love and understanding of beauty, from achievements of art and imaginative understanding to the cultivation of curiosity and free inquiry into the civilizations of the past. These are the things toward which great civilizations move as their true end and meaning. Practical economic and political matters are essential to a society's survival but are subordinate to these activities and experiences. Experiences formerly associated with the humanities and liberal arts have degenerated into entertainment to be indulged in during our brief respite from the drudgery of participation in technological production. (For an interesting discussion of the scientific world view that influences these sentiments and experiences, see Paul Feyerabend, *The Conquest of Abundance: A Tale of Abstraction versus the Richness of Being* [Chicago: The University of Chicago Press, 1999]).

Thus, the third strand of educational ideas is traced through John Dewey, who in 1938 was imploring educators and reformers not just to place the experience of the learning *being* at the centre of education but to do so for democratic purposes and for the larger good of young people and society. Indeed, learning and education were posited as fundamentally social and political processes. But the ways in which education is fundamentally social, political, and surrounding the experiences of young people requires thought. Dewey's political and critical statements have been built upon by numerous other critical pedagogues, including Paulo Freire and sociologists and historians of youth. This work also demonstrates the ways in which schools can become a source of social problems, contrary to their real purposes, by holding many young people back and reproducing the inequalities that exist in society.

Jean Anyon's early ethnographic studies of social reproduction in schools continue to be important today. In the 1980s, Anyon began to examine how social class is reproduced in school experiences and practices of curriculum, pedagogy, and school governance, asserting that schooling is too often a springboard to nothing more than preparation to take one's place in the socially stratified society. The schools she studied appeared to be doing two things. First, they were preparing young people for a particular type of working life upon leaving school. Second, they were channelling young people into jobs of similar occupational levels and social classes as those held by their parents. These occupational levels ranged from high status (upper-class, the corporate president level) to relatively lower status (working class or working poor). For Anyon and other critical pedagogues, these practices constitute a hidden curriculum of school.

Anyon (1980) also illustrates how teachers invoke this hidden curriculum. For example, those in working-class schools tend to hold low expectations for students and to discourage thinking about novel ways of doing things. Instead, school tasks are standardized or mechanistic: 'work is following the steps of a procedure' (p. 363). Anyon contrasts this with the situation in upper-middle-class schools where 'work is creative activity carried out independently' (p. 370). The underlying philosophy is that people engaged in 'low-level' repetitive work do not need to think or innovate, while 'professionals' are required to do so daily. Indeed, the working-class schools used a banking model of education as described by Paulo Freire in *Pedagogy of the Oppressed* (1970). Here, rote learning and transmission of technical knowledge are the sole modes of teaching. Practices of gearing schools to occupational and technical expectations are discriminatory. Stated simply, the education system can be accused of depriving many youth of the type of schooling that would allow them to gain a meaningful education and to compete in the marketplace for middle-class jobs. But, it is not only social class inequality that is reproduced in schools.

George Smith's (1998) work in the Canadian context also illustrates how schools are socially organized to reproduce homophobia and create very negative climates for gay students. In speaking to secondary school students in Toronto, Ontario, Smith produced *The Ideology of the 'Fag'*, which outlines the ways in which schools are biased against homosexual youth on multiple levels. Schools, he suggests, are set up in a hegemonic way wherein teachers and other students give heterosexual students more power than homosexual students. He traces the processes through which this ideology is established and describes how homosexual students begin to feel afraid to be themselves and to become fearful social outcasts. Physical abuse, emotional abuse, and fear become a part of their everyday school experiences. Indeed, current research shows that young gay and bisexual men are more likely to attempt suicide than their heterosexual counterparts (cf., Youth Suicide Problems, Gay/Bisexual Male Focus, www. youth-suicide.com/gay-bisexual, Tremblay, 2010).

Thus, schools are doing much better by some young people than others and not all schools are the same. Schools tend to get caught up in the act of circling back to meeting the needs of modern technological society. This excludes serious debate and discussion about what school ought to be as an emerging social institution and the primary container of modern youth. At present, the Canadian Education Association (CEA) is attempting to place both of these ideas at the centre of a national conversation and debate about the future of schools and young people.

In these three trains of thinking about education, three follies of contemporary education are seen. First, education becomes a form of 'training' for a select few and a form of true 'education' for even fewer. Second, too many young people are left behind at the very time their human and societal enhancement is at stake. Thus, the place of schools in the social marginalization of youth becomes a serious debate. And, third, the confusion between 'schooling' and 'education' continues. *Modernity's Youth: Images of Rebellion from the Cave* (Srigley & Tilleczek, 2008) tracks these follies as originally conceived in Plato's *Republic* with more recent reverberations into modern American cinema and the lives of youth. Indeed, youth become prisoners of the cave in which only shadows and images appear; or, as Dewey asserts, school is about *seeming* and appearance and not about authentic experience and *being*. Education becomes ever more elusive in a system of modern technological schooling.

Young People Speak about Education and Schools

When asked, young people themselves speak about straddling the tensions of modern schooling and while they may not like 'school', they opt for a critical and engaged path to education. Current Canadian research with young people and educators shows that the differences between school and education are well recognized by young people but not so well recognized by educators. The concepts of schooling and education are often conflated. Young people tell us that even though they may feel marginalized from the daily structures and practices of modern *schools* and learning processes, may struggle academically, or may leave school early, they still see a value and place for themselves in *education* (Tilleczek, 2008a, d). They may not wish to return to their high schools per se, but seek instead to gain the experience, knowledge, and social outcomes of education. This is an important distinction. Recent social scientific literatures and our discussions with over 800 young people regarding their lives at school, in homes, and in communities provide enduring evidence of youth in want of relevant and passionate education that acknowledges their experiences and *being* while providing a solid process of *becoming* and working toward their imagined future. School also is a place of *belonging*.

Youth actively negotiate their lives in and across modern schools and while they may leave school as an act of rebellion or to feed a family, they perceive this as a wise choice, an informed act. For those who leave school as an act of rebellion, the act of leaving is often conceived to be against school but when questioned these youth have stated that they also have a love of and need for education. In many cases, the types of schools that these 'dropout' students encountered were overly technical, rational, inflexible, and lacking in passionate and relevant content and pedagogy. Moreover, the entrenchment of pathological and psychological models of youth means that school 'dropouts' remain characterized as de-contextualized deviants who individually and wrongly decide to leave school and create problems for themselves and society.

However, social scientists have learned that the processes of disengagement from school begin prior to the act of school withdrawal and are related to countless events and experiences, and complex chains of narrative events. And virtually all of the young people who left school early with whom we spoke in 2005 stated that they would return to finish their education:

> Reducing levels of educational attrition requires a focus, first and fore-most, on the curriculum and on patterns of teacher–student interaction, underpinned by an understanding of subjective interpretations of the place of education and the ways in which approaches are mediated by cultural orientations and priorities. Indeed, while institutional frameworks are badly in need of repair and often ill-suited to the contexts of late modernity, any significant reduction in disengagement requires a more advanced understanding of the complex relationship between cultures internal and external to the school. Serious and persistent patterns of underachievement can be reduced by reforming the curriculum but equal opportunities are dependent on more far-reaching policy reform. (Furlong, 2008: 2)

Another Canadian Educational Paradox

There is an additional paradox occurring in Canadian education. Indeed, 25 per cent of the students across Organization for Economic Co-Operation and Development (OECD) countries are said to be unhappy with their schools (Willms, 2003) and only 37 per cent of Canadian students have been found to be intellectually engaged at school (Willms, Freisen, & Milton, 2009). Indeed, overall levels of engagement in school were found to be quite low when measured as social, academic, and intellectual engagement. And levels of academic engagement fall steadily from grade 6 to grade 12 in Canada (Willms et al., 2009). In 2000, over half (56 per cent) of students aged 10 to 15 said they liked school very much or quite a bit. But school was less popular with 14- and 15-year-olds than with younger children. In 1998, a higher proportion of *both* older and younger students said they liked school than did those in 2000 (CCSD, 2006). Moreover, socio-economic status remained related to student engagement with young people from high and very high socio-economic backgrounds having significantly higher levels of engagement and a more positive sense of belonging at school (Willms et al., 2009). Across Canada, many students in both 1996 and 2000 said their teachers did treat them fairly (58 per cent of those aged 10 to 15); not surprisingly, students who felt their teachers were not treating them fairly were less likely to say they liked school or were doing well at it. These students were also less likely to aspire to university. However, 88 per cent of Canadian students aged 10 to 15 aspired to post-secondary educations, with 40 per cent hoping for a university degree and 28 per cent aspiring to more than one degree. As was the case in 1996, students from households with incomes over $40,000 per year were more likely than lower-income students to say they hoped to get at least one university degree, and girls were more likely than boys to say that they wanted to get more than one degree (Canadian Council on Social Development, 2006).

We can witness trends whereby increasing numbers of youth in Canada are indeed completing high school and participating in post-secondary education but many others are not. In 2002, more than three-quarters (77 per cent) of young adults aged 20 to 24 had achieved some post-secondary education—up from 72 per cent in 1994. Just 11 per cent of this group had less than a high school education, down from 14 per cent in 1994. Young men were more likely than women to have less than a high school education (13 per cent compared to 8 per cent). Young women were more likely to have at least some post-secondary education (82 per cent versus 74 per cent of young men), and they were twice as likely to have a degree (12 per cent compared to 6 per cent). Young men and women were equally likely to have obtained a post-secondary certificate or diploma by the age of 24 (Canada Council on Social Development, 2008). But there are still many gaps in levels of achievement of the post-secondary educations required for good stead in modern society. If so many are aspiring to post-secondary school yet many are disengaging from their secondary schools, who is left out and what are the processes by which this social marginalization is taking place? Poverty, gender, and cultural background remain as serious out-of-school factors that continue to create marginality.

A recent response in the United States regarding former president Bush's No Child Left Behind (NCLB) act recognized its limits as a social policy to address these issues. Berliner notes that,

> some of the most distinguished educators in the nation have joined
> together to promote a broader, bolder approach to education. The

potential effectiveness of NCLB has been seriously undermined by its acceptance of the popular assumptions that bad schools are the major reason for low achievement, and that an academic program revolving around standards, testing, teacher training, and accountability can, in and of itself, offset the full impact of low socioeconomic status on achievement. (2009: 5)

As the complex culturing nesting approach suggests, both in- *and* out-of-school factors must be considered at multiple levels:

At the same time, to tackle effectively disengagement we need to recognise that accommodating cultural complexity and ensuring the engagement of young learners will not in itself solve the problem of high school drop outs. Irrespective of levels of commitment, some will have to leave due to family issues and those experiencing household poverty may need to earn a wage at an early stage. For these reasons it is important to make disengagement a redundant term through the development of new, more fluid, educational pathways in which opportunities are not linked to age. (Furlong, 2008: 2)

What are the known in-school factors and experiences in which the physical, academic, and social selves of youth may be fostered or hindered? If we are to insist that young people spend their days from the ages of 4 to 24 in the presence of same-aged peers in public education classrooms, it is important to know how they are functioning. In the most positive sense, schools should exist to educate students to be fully functioning members of a democratic society. And, in my ongoing research relating to schools as told from the point of view of young people, educators, and parents, three themes repeat themselves:

1. The value of making deep human connections between educators, youth, and their friends.
2. The need for further understanding and debate about the cultures of youth and the aims of school (e.g., determining what education is for, what works and what does not from the point of view of schooled youth and schooled society).
3. The need for a clearer understanding of the struggles of contemporary schooled young people in modern and technological contexts.

In short, the fundamental social processes of *being, becoming,* and *belonging* reverberate in the stories and voices of young people in schools.

But schools are not the same in addressing these social processes, and the aims of schools alter with political and social understandings about young people. As Davies and Guppy (2006) put it, the paradox of a schooled society is that it serves more and more young people for longer periods of time and in so doing, creates an ongoing potential for disenfranchisement. Thus, the examination of schools and education must attend to the ways in which marginalization occurs and is organized in the very institutions that claim to liberate and educate. As we discussed briefly, a compelling starting point in examining education and youth is from the point of view of those who have disengaged from it and have left school before completing their diploma. This view from the margins of schools provides an often neglected space for examining how school is understood, experienced, put together, organized, and governed. These voices act as 'a timely reminder that it is time to re-engage and develop our knowledge of a process that underpins social stratification and reinforces cycles of disadvantage' (Furlong, 2008: 2).

Two recent Canadian studies of the culture of schooling serve to exemplify some of these issues (see Tilleczek, 2008d and Tilleczek et al., 2010). In the first, the goal was to conduct a large-scale, ethnographic study of the lived experience of disengagement from school. The collective and composite testimonials of these students were presented in Chapter 1. In the second project the research team continued this work to better understand the place of the transition from elementary to secondary school as both fresh starts and false starts for youth. These studies were conducted to better understand students in context of risk situations and protective factors experienced at school and communities. Both studies also aimed to look at the culture of schools and the larger economic and political realities that contribute to the issues of disengagement and early leaving, and the processes of schooling and education for contemporary young people.

As was stated in Chapter 1, the cultural nesting approach attends to all levels but lends a focus to the meso-level practices—in this case the schools and families—where the culture and individual come together. Not surprisingly, in these studies the protective factors encountered (although the young people spoke of fewer positive than negative factors) were mirror images of the problems that were encountered. This interrelation between barriers and facilitators at school was of interest. For example, some educators were able to forge excellent school–home links that facilitated the support and care of students. Others were less proactive, and many were seen as uncaring. A flexible administration was one that recognized the need for open doors for many youth to allow for false starts and re-entry points. Table 6.1 provides additional examples of risk factors that young people bring with them to school and/or that occur within the school.

In both studies, policy makers and educators were advised that the young people in the process of disengagement were asking for them to be more *proactive*, *caring*, and *flexible* in their practices; the policy makers and educators were also advised to recognize the homogeneity and complexity of the everyday

Table 6.1 Risk Situations for Leaving School Early

Risk Factors	Culture and Society	Classroom and Homes	Youth and Teachers
Beyond school	Social class (poverty) and socio-economic gradients Minority group status Gender 'Place' (region) Immigration/resettlement	Family styles School–Home link Adult status (need to work and/or care for families, etc.); relates to socio-economic status	Disabilities Social isolation Identity struggles Moves/interruptions
Within school	Lack of referral or outreach to other agencies outside the school Negative school cultures Negative administrator relations Lack of assessment for disabilities School culture conflicts	Ineffective discipline Negative teacher–student relations (expectations) Irrelevant curriculum Passive instruction Disregard for student Lack of support in school or outreach to others outside of the school	Low levels of engagement in school Academic/social struggles Suspensions/retentions

Source: Tilleczek, 2008.

lives of the young people who were disengaging from school. Indeed, Willms et al. (2009) also found that there was a great deal of variability among schools in their ability to engage students, with secondary schools having the lowest levels of sense of belonging, attendance, and intellectual engagement. Similar to Tilleczek (2008d), this study further reported that the meso-level factors in the classroom and schools had strong effects on student engagement. High teacher expectations, positive student–teacher relations, and appropriate levels of instructional challenges were all important. In fact, over one-half of the variation among schools on student belonging, attendance, and intellectual engagement was attributed by Willms and his team to classroom and school learning climate (Willms, 2009). Further to this, schools that had higher levels of socio-economic status (SES) had fewer students who suffered from a low sense of belonging but did not necessarily show higher levels of intellectual engagement: 'In other words, SES is related to participation and intellectual engagement within most schools, but schools with higher levels of SES do not necessarily have higher levels of these types of engagement' (Willms et al., 2009: 26). It is classroom and school climate that play a much more important role in variation by social class. As in the Ontario Transitions Study (Tilleczek et al., 2009) the young people moving into high school felt like outsiders if they perceived their social class (or the amount of money their families had) to be less in comparison to the other students in their school. Social comparison and its incumbent problems require further examination.

Therefore, not all schools are the same and not all educators are up to the challenges of understanding and intervening in problems facing modern youth cultures. Moreover, schools are integral for youth due to their place in the complex cultural nests and the community of beings that exists there. But these beings exist outside the walls of schools, in informal educational settings and with friends and families. Schools alone cannot position our youth for their futures. In fact, in 2009, only 42 per cent of Canadian students felt confident in their language arts skills. There is a need for broader understanding of the cultural and political contexts within which these social and intellectual connections proliferate or falter. There is a need for further understanding of the fundamental social processes of being, becoming, and belonging in the contexts of schools and communities. What are the aims of modern schooling and how are these shifting aims directly and indirectly influencing schooled youth in schooled societies? What are the roles of families and friends in enhancing or negating the important social processes of being, becoming, and belonging in the lives of young people?

Families and Friends: A Great Debate

Families, friends, and peer groups extend the social webs that surround young people. One of the great debates in youth studies is the relative impact and importance of families and friends at this stage of life. It is true that when high school students in Canada were asked to indicate what was very important to them, 85 per cent cited friends and 'freedom' at the top of their lists (CCSD, 2006). Popular opinion, media representations, and parental comments often centre around the idea that young people wish *only* to spend time with their friends and will no longer 'listen' to their parents and other adults. These adults seem 'geeky' in comparison. Most Hollywood films, television shows, and advertisements portray the loud, confident, and cocky young person confronting the out-of-date, snivelling adult who has no clue about the contemporary world in which young people live. The idea of the generation gap looms large today just as Bob Dylan so aptly pointed out in the 1960s.

This idea of change is a good entrance into the examination of families and friends since both social settings have undergone rapid shifts in the past decades. As well, the shifting and bumpy character of social relationships with parents, siblings, and friends is a central part of the lives of young people. But does the increase in value and time spent with friends necessarily translate into poor relationships with families? Do all young people have strained relationships with their parents and discount their advice and input? What roles do families and friends serve in the lives of young people, and how does this relate to their education? These are the questions that will be addressed in this section.

Young people and their friends/peers separate themselves from children and adults to form distinct cultures that consist of separate images (fashion, hair, tattoos, etc.), demeanours (gestures, postures, etc.), and argot (vocabulary, jargon, etc.) (Brake, 1985). Since 1994, data in Canada has shown that over 90 per cent of young people said they had many friends. Girls were slightly more likely than boys to feel this way, and family income made no difference (CCSD, 2006). However, data from the National Longitudinal Survey of Children and Youth (NLSCY) shows that when faced with a situation that needed discussion, young people said they were most likely to talk to their mothers (83 per cent) or fathers (62 per cent) about problems. Only 32 per cent of young people aged 10 to 13 said they had no problems with their friends. Forty-three per cent said the same about their mothers, and 45 per cent said they had no problems with their fathers. Only 20 per cent said they got along very well with their siblings. The data clearly reflects that there are many young people who perceive problems within their relationships with family and friends. This community of beings is important, but not without real challenges. Moreover, these relationships are nested within the larger community setting and a sense of belonging to one's community is associated with higher levels of health (CIHI, 2006). Fortunately, the data from the Canadian Community Health Survey indicate that almost three-quarters (72 per cent) of Canadian youth aged 12 to 19 felt a sense of belonging to their community. The plot thickens such that friends and families are important but often troubling while communities are important and relatively welcoming of youth.

It is well known that establishing friendships is fundamental to positive youth development and that those with close friends tend to have better social and academic outcomes. When asked what gave them a great deal/quite a bit of enjoyment, the young people surveyed indicated that friends again topped the list (94 per cent), followed by music (90 per cent) (Bibby, 2001). However, this is also true of having close ties to families. A joint World Health Organization and Health Canada study, *Trends in the Health of Canadian Youth* (2004), found that, overall, grade 10 students who had a more positive relationship with their parents were more likely to be satisfied with their lives. Parental support was also found to be important to students' confidence and their aspirations. Among Canadian students who said their parents were always ready to help, 32 per cent felt they were doing very well in school, 21 per cent liked school very much, and 72 per cent hoped to get at least a university degree (CCSD,

2006). It is fair to conclude that while the character of relationships changes for young people, the need to have strong and supportive friends and families remains stable. The continuities and discontinuities in each sphere are worth exploring.

In the case of families, what has changed is the structure of the family such that only 68 per cent of Canadian young people in 2001 had biological parents who were married to each other. However, most Canadian youth continue to report having a happy home life but there is a reported small decrease in happiness as they get older such that by grade 10, 15 per cent fewer girls said they were happy with their lives at home than was the case in grade 6. The majority of students across the grades felt trusted by their parents, valued what their parents thought of them, and desired parental approval. There are, however, clear gender differences in relationships with parents. For example, more boys than girls in grades 6 to 10 said their parents understood them. Older girls—those in grades 8 and 10—were less likely to say their parents understood and trusted them; they were less satisfied with their home life, had more arguments, and more desire to leave home. Some conflict with parents appears to be inevitable as youth move toward independence (CCSD, 2006). Such gender differences are likely related to a complex interplay and interaction between genders across generations as well as varying understanding of sons and daughters.

The discontinuities in friendships and peer patterns have been noted over historical time and across the years as young people age. However, as Bibby has exclaimed, 'it would be difficult to overestimate the role of friendships in teenage lives' (Bibby, 2001: 50). For instance, in one study of the transition from elementary to secondary school, young people report that while friends were always very important, the character of the relationships was less 'dramatic' as they left secondary school (Tilleczek et al., 2009). However, upon entering high school, friends were seen as both a resource and a potential distraction from both social and academic matters. Two quotations from young people illustrate the point:

> It's really distracting. Like one of my classes, I have a lot of friends in it, we all sit in one group, so we always get in trouble because they're always talking. And . . . we're texting back and forth.

> Yeah, my Grade Twelve friends they, 'cuz they've been in the school for four years now so they helped me and they told me everything I need to know . . . Like, where the classes are, they told me like, directions and everything and they told me like, what teachers are really good [laughter] and ones that they don't like, and they told me about the programs, too. (Tilleczek et al., 2009: 114)

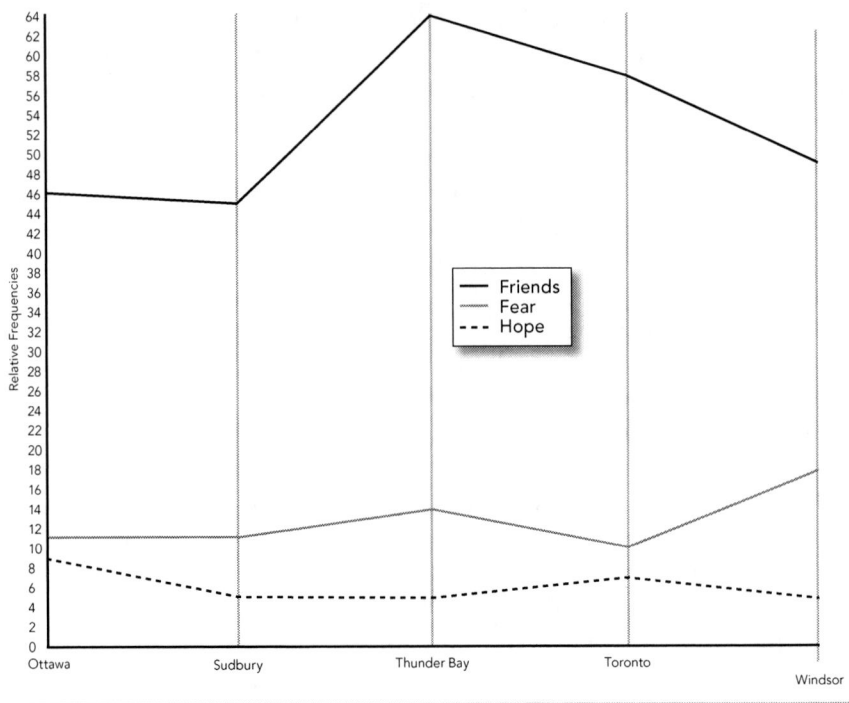

Figure 6.1: Grade 8 Youth (Elementary School) Relative Frequencies of the Importance of Friends, Hopes, and Fears on Transitioning into High School

Source: Tilleczek, Laflamme, et al., 2009.

What remained stable, however, was the importance of friends. Figures 6.1 and 6.2 illustrate grade 8 and grade 9 plots for the relative frequency of importance of friends, fear, and hope for young people in Ontario, Canada, as based on in-depth interviews with 42 young people in grade 8 and 62 young people in grade 9. It is noteworthy that there was not much change in the frequencies across diverse regions of the province.

Families also have held continuities and discontinuities in their relationships with young people over historical time, across cultures, and as their children come of age. It is clear that familial institutions have experienced many changes in the last decades of modernity. These changes amount to alterations in the number of siblings and the character of caregivers that young people have access to. What is continuous, regardless of familial structural changes and who is providing care, is the constant need for supportive and loving caregivers. Indeed, it is the main source of longer-term and ongoing support and modelling for youth. Young people tend to emulate their parents' value systems relating to substantial issues about politics and education while they

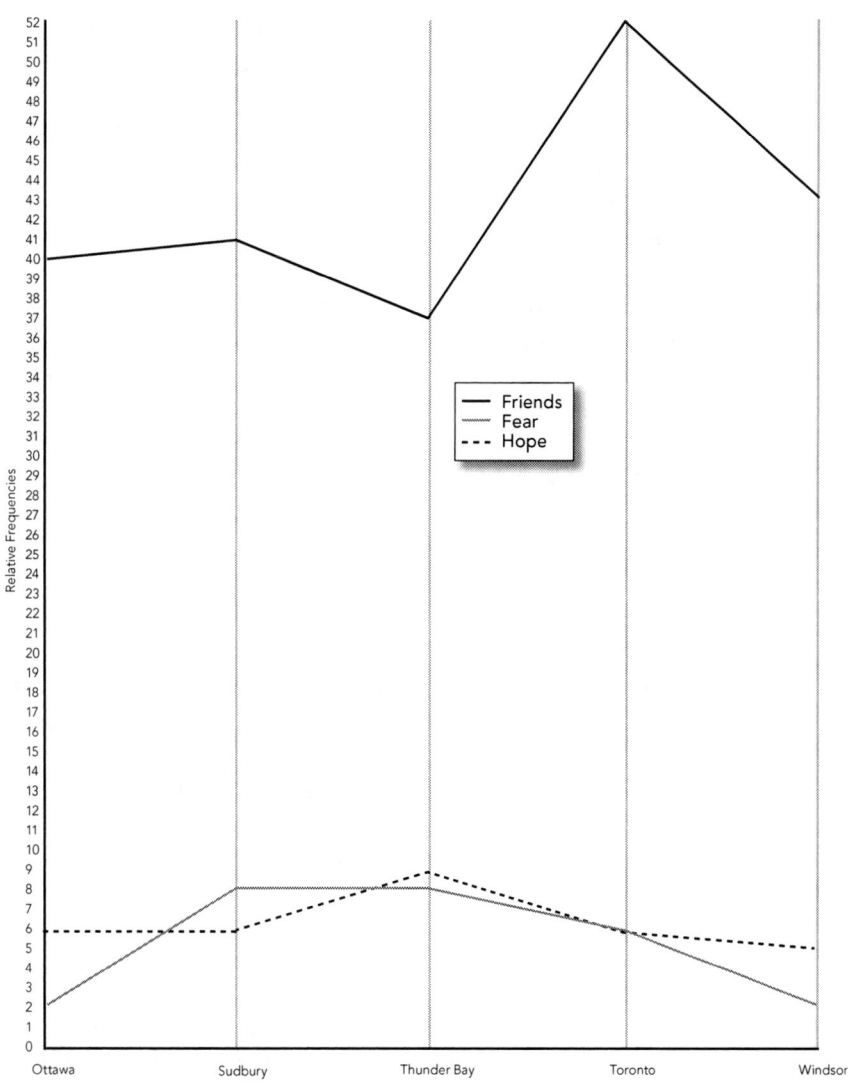

Figure 6.2: Grade 9 Youth (Secondary School) Relative Frequencies of the Importance of Friends, Hopes, and Fears on Transitioning into High School

Source: Tilleczek, Laflamme, et al., 2009.

emulate their friends and peers in more fleeting issues relating to fashion and fads.

Becoming competent adults is a long-term process that is most often gradual but also marked by periods of rapid development and reorganization (Case, 1991). Optimal home environments are those that foster young people through critical developmental transitions (Keating, 1996), and have in them secure and loving attachments with nurturing adults (Suomi, 1999).

Social connections and the perception of control over one's life are also protective factors against later health problems (Kiecolt-Glaser et al., 1995). The factors most influential in protecting vulnerable youth are considerable individual attention, and a society that is able to support families and schools (Keating, 1996). In a study of young people during the transitional years it was found that parents of students in grade 9 were fairly well informed about what was going on in the lives of their sons and daughters (Tilleczek, Laflamme, et al., 2009). However, parents were not informed to the same extent across school work, extracurricular activities, and friends. Indeed, the closer they moved toward asking about friends, or the further away they moved from asking about school-related activities, the more reluctant young people were to let their parents know about their activities. School was the domain in which parents were the most informed, followed by extracurricular activities, followed by activities with friends (Tilleczek, Laflamme, et al., 2009).

What changes over time is the character of the relationship since both parents and young people are in flux. These shifts in the relationship require extra advocacy and thought as parents attempt to support their sons and daughters in different ways as they age. Parents report (Tilleczek, Laflamme, et al., 2009) how they found it challenging but important to remain aware and supportive of their children's school work over the course of their transition into high school. For example, two separate parents nicely summed up hundreds of pages of discussion group transcripts and the main elements of this great debate of shifting parent-youth relationships by stating this:

> Yeah, I would say it's a different role because like in grade school, it's like she would just come more naturally, like more trust like, you were more involved with decisions made that she would try to make whereas at this level now, it's like very important that she make the decisions and you know, there's that tug of war thing [between] mother-daughter like she's going to if I make that decision then no, it's definitely like if you don't have to be the opposite so it's like I definitely don't want to be making her decisions you know, let her have that room but yet she has to know that she can't make all the decisions, I mean she's only fifteen. So yeah, to like be supportive so it's a little different than in the grade school. You know, still having to be there and if it's something heavy then she can come to you, she doesn't have to handle it or decide it but for the most part you know, just trying to give her that room, eh? So I find it's a bit of a trick.

> I knew that this was only grade nine and depending on how far this teacher went, I would step in. But I wanted to give him some space to be able to react and to see the different types of teachers and be able to

react 'cause if I stepped in I mean, grade nine for sure, there could be one in grade ten, grade eleven, grade twelve, and he wouldn't know how to respond to something like that. So I would just make sure to reinforce that you know . . . don't be afraid or think that you're tattle-taling on him, just tell me . . . and we'll talk to him, it doesn't have to be a big thing, whatever. . . . But you know I probably would have gotten more involved, why did this happen, why wasn't I called, why wasn't I—But I've, I've learned that I kind of have to step back a little bit in high school because this is where the transition starts. Like in three years, he could be gone from the house, he could be, you know—and if I keep on having too much control then he won't know how to, how to react in society. . . .' (Tilleczek, Laflamme, et al., 2009: 135)

Critical Thinking Activities

1. There is no shortage of media coverage about education and schools. Examine four different sources of media (TV, radio, magazines, and newspapers) and look for evidence of a) the irony of modern schools and b) the education/school blunder.
2. Search the Canadian Vanier Institute of the Family website (www.vifamily. ca/) and note its definition of *family*. Can you think of any type of family that would not be included in this definition? Can you think of a better definition? Find five interesting statistics about Canadian families that may impact young people from the site.
3. How would you study youth friendships today? Where would the study take place and why? How would you integrate digital cultures into your work?

Further Readings

Anyon, J. (1980). Social class and the hidden curriculum of work. *Journal of Education, 162*, 67–92.

Davies, S. & Guppy, N. (2006). *The Schooled Society*. Toronto: Oxford University Press.

Dewey, J. (1938). *Experience and Education*. New York: Touchstone Press.

Freire, P. (1970). *Pedagogy of the Oppressed*. New York: Continuum.

Suggested Websites

Canadian Education Association (CEA)
http://cea-ace.ca/home.cfm

Early School Leavers Study
www.edu.gov.on.ca/eng/parents/schoolleavers.pdf

The Vanier Institute of the Family
www.vifamily.ca/

Youth Suicide Problems: Gay/Bisexual Male Focus
www.youth-suicide.com/gay-bisexual

Part Four

Mirrors and Passages: Being a Modern Youth

This final section of the book consists of two chapters. Chapter 7 aims to explore the fundamental social processes of *being* for young people and in youth studies. The chapter unpacks the ideas of identity and social passage through the important but contested concepts of risk and resilience and, from a cultural nesting approach, examines some specific examples of social acts of passages, such as smoking, driving, and making friends. One of the mains points of Chapter 7 is to address the need and space for positive development, resistance, and agency in youth studies and the chapter does this by further exploring narrative and biography as means for studying social processes of *being*.

Chapter 8 builds on this momentum and provides examples of policy, practice, and action *with*, *for*, and *by* youth. These actions speak to the being and becoming of youth and how society treats them. The important ideas about research with and for young people are reiterated in an attempt to address a reflective, evidence-based practice in youth studies. Both social policy and social action are considered and exemplified with a range of youth social actions and movements from anti-globalization to civil rights activism. This section of the book then concludes with critical summarizing statements about an emerging youth studies.

Chapter Seven

The Joys and Challenges of Being: Is There an Optimal Youth?

Let me put it more clearly, since no one will believe that a thirteen-year-old girl is completely alone in the world. And I'm not. I have loving parents and a sixteen-year-old sister and about thirty people that I can call friends. And I have a throng of admirers who can't keep their eyes off me and have to resort to using a broken pocket mirror to try to catch a glimpse of me in the classroom. I have a family, loving aunts and a good home. No, on the surface I seem to have everything, except my one true friend . . . That is why I have started the diary. (Anne Frank, *The Diary of a Young Girl*, 1991: 6)

*'We **are** rich,' said Anne staunchly. 'Why, we have sixteen years to our credit, and we're happy as queens, and we've all got imaginations, more or less. Look at that sea, girls—all silver and shallow and a vision of things not seen. We couldn't enjoy the loveliness any more if we had millions of dollars and ropes of diamonds. You wouldn't change into any of these women if you could. Would you want to be that white-lace girl and wear a sour look all your life, as if you'd been turning up your nose at the world?'* (L.M. Montgomery, *Anne of Green Gables*, 1908)

Introduction

This chapter examines the fundamental social processes of *being* a young person: the experiences and processes of identity and self-formation. Modernity and identity are two current preoccupations in social sciences generally and in youth studies specifically. While they cannot be separated, the focus here is on *being* in the modern context, how identity has been understood, and the outcomes of this work. Erik Erikson's early work of the 1950s and 1960s in psychosocial development has had an immense influence on current understandings of youth identity. His descriptions of the processes whereby young people work to sort out identity formation versus role confusion and his use of biographical and psychoanalytical methods are noteworthy. Erikson surmised identity formation to be the most critical work of youth. This chapter traces selected paths arising from his direction.

In recent years there has been a surge of work arising from psychology about young people as essentially individuals who exhibit many 'problem' behaviours and overindulge in negative and dangerous experiences. This pervasive idea has arisen from a model of youth as deviant or troubled risk-takers, suggesting that problems arise outside of the political and economic climate of youth culture. As Schissel (2007) theorizes, deviance has been sold to us by the media, who are determined to sell papers rather than to reflect the realities of youth culture. In addition, the 'at-risk' discussions that permeate the fields of education and counselling lead us to policies and practices that target individual youth rather than focusing on 'in-risk' situations from which they come and attempt to negotiate (Tilleczek et al., 2010). Youth identity is therefore another location of fallacious notions of individual process that eclipse the cultural and social character of such (Furlong & Cartmel, 2007).

A recent review of international literature (Tilleczek & Ferguson, 2007) revealed the importance of the concept of living *in risk situations*, rather than simply conceptualizing individual youth themselves to be *at risk* and thus the location of risk. Some researchers understand risk as a simple statistical probability where high risk carries high odds for problematic outcomes (Luthar, 2006). But risk status should also be conceived of as fluctuating over time, based on circumstances and contexts, rather than being a fixed quality. Many think that risk is better understood as a point along a continuum (Schonert-Reichl, 2000; Catterall, 1998) or as depicting a situation rather than an individual and, in fact, recommend the use of the phrase 'students in at-risk situations' (Smink & Schargel, 2004). But more than a simple continuum or host of situations is required to attend to the cultural nests within which identity is played out.

Periods of age-related, social, or economic transition can increase situations of risk for young people as they necessitate individual and institutional adaptive capabilities (Schonert-Reichl, 2000). If a young person faces multiple negative factors at home, at school, and in the neighbourhood, the effect of these factors is multiplied rather than simply added together because these conditions interact with and reinforce each other (Werner & Smith, 1992; Schorr, 1989). In situations where youth are vulnerable, the interaction of risk and protective factors determines a course of development. If multiple risk factors accumulate and are not offset by compensating protective factors, healthy development is compromised (Schorr, 1989; Werner & Smith, 1992). For example, Garbarino (1990) describes high-risk neighbourhoods as an ecological conspiracy against youth. Poverty increases the likelihood that risk factors in the environment will not be offset by protective factors. In fact, poverty has been seen by some as a constellation of risks that combine to produce 'rotten outcomes' (Schorr, 1989: 3).

It is therefore necessary to unpack ideas about 'normal', 'pathological', 'risk', and 'resilience' and to be aware of the use of these terms in contemporary youth studies. The media, consumers, government, academics, and police each play a role in producing moral panics and making folk-devils of youth (Schissel, 2007). This is not to say that all young people are exempt from atrocious behaviour. But the conversations relating to the socially contextualized place of risk and resilience must be heeded. Chapter 2 has already provided a brief history of the emergence of negative images of youth. This chapter begins with a brief history of the competing ideas of resiliency and positive youth development. It then turns to research relating to the experiences of social relationships, smoking, and driving. The chapter ends with a discussion of biography and narrative as a process for understanding the complex cultural nests within which modern youth negotiate experiences and form identities.

Resilience: Promises and Pathways for Youth

The concept of resilience has been discussed for the past 40 years in North America and is currently experiencing a surge of interest. For example, in November of 2008 some 400 Canadians attended a National Dialogue on Resilience in Youth hosted by the Canadian Council on Learning. Far from reaching a clear consensus on the use and importance of the concept, the dialogue examined issues of policy, theory, methods, and applications of resilience. *Resilience* was defined as 'a phenomenon or process reflecting relatively positive adaptation despite experiences of significant adversity or trauma' (Luthar, 2006: 742). Luthar also suggests that the two distinct dimensions—significant adversity and positive adaptation—are those that are actually measured and that resiliency is therefore inferred from these two measures. Forms of adversity most often studied are exposure to violence, maternal depression, and poverty, or composite risks such as parents' low income and/or histories of mental illness (Luthar, 2003).

The nuances added to this definition by Ungar (2008) illustrate that individual strengths and resilience are related but not the exactly the same. Strengths are a wide set of internal and external assets experienced by young people. The more assets a young person has, the more likely she is to succeed in culturally sanctioned ways. Common strengths were grouped under the following categories: parental support and expectations; positive peer relationships; community cohesiveness; commitment to learning at school; school culture (bonding and high expectations by educators); cultural sensitivity; self-control; empowerment (including safety); strong self-concept; and social sensitivity (empathy and social justice). Resilience, on the other hand, describes the presence of these strengths when young people are exposed to multiple risks.

Ungar (2008) provides a further distinction between common and hidden resilience. He states that we commonly understand resilience to indicate coping in ways that are valued by those who represent the dominant culture (mental health professionals, educators, etc.). A young person who, despite exposure to multiple risks, stays in school and acts age appropriately is understood to be resilient. But some young people cope as best they can with their strengths in an environment that does not offer many other ways to succeed. Rather than seeing such behaviour as necessarily dysfunctional it can be seen as *hidden resilience*. This suggests that the young person is making due with the strengths she does have (defiance, missing school, etc.) in order to cope in a neglectful environment. For example, the Early School Leavers Study demonstrated that young people's leaving school was a sign of coping given the cultural nests within which they found themselves (Tilleczek, 2008d). It is important to recognize and measure *the fit* between an individual's capacity to cope (strengths), the risks she faces, and the context in which this takes place (is the school/home/community environment supportive or does it burden the child?) since all are integral to whether resilience can be expected or not (Unger, 2008; Tilleczek et al., 2009):

> Where once we spoke of 'beating the odds' stacked against a child, there is growing evidence that resilience is just as much about 'changing the odds' so that children thrive. The most common image of resilience promoted by those in the psychological sciences is of a strong child who interacts well with a diminished environment, achieving outcomes thought exceptional. The view is of the rugged individual. A bi-ocular view of the problem of resilience is more accurate. Individuals adapt *to the extent that environments provide them with what they need.* To identify a 'resilient individual' is a misnomer. An individual is resilient only to the extent he finds among his family and community the resources he needs to develop the internal strengths that are associated with experiences of resilience. External resources in one or more areas of a child's life help make up for the challenges the child faces in the areas of his life that function less well (keeping in mind that resilience only describes children who experience adversity). (Ungar, 2008: 6)

The concepts of resilience, adaptation, and protective factors are the positive counterparts to adversity, vulnerability, and risk. Resilient youth are those who remain competent despite exposure to misfortune or stressful events (Werner & Smith, 1992). Caring and support, high expectations, and opportunities for meaningful participation are protective factors for children found in families, schools, and communities (Keating & Hertzman, 1999). One important protective factor for children is the availability of consistent adults who provide them with a secure base for the development of trust, autonomy, and initiative (Werner & Smith, 1992).

Catterall (1998) suggests a unique and practical signpost in our use of risk and resilience. He suggests that risk be assessed as grounded in actual performance rather than assessed by abstract categories relating to various group-level probabilities of failure. In studying grade 8 students over time in the US, he found that those who were doing poorly in school could turn themselves around by grade 10. Family supports, school responsiveness to student needs, and student involvement in school were shown to be strong predictors of student recovery from low school performance. He goes on to suggest that we should avoid seeing all members of risk groups as necessarily 'at risk' without also seeing the potential for resilience within families and schools. Resilience, therefore, can be experienced in the ways in which families and schools help students to recover from low performance, lack of confidence, and faltering commitments to school:

> One potential response of group labelling is that individual children
> may be considered at risk who are in fact not at risk; after all, roughly
> half the students will exceed any group average . . . In addition, a key
> proposition supported in the resilience research is that individuals react
> differently to their surroundings . . . in a way, risk may be a positive spark
> for some children, and a central quest of resilience research has been to
> discover who really is (or is not) at risk in an adversely predicted group.
> Another effect . . . is that through stereotyping, expectations for entire
> groups may be suppressed with unfortunate educational consequence
> (Oakes, 1985). Finally, some popular conceptions of risk for children
> should be challenged because risk by association can translate into guilt
> by association. In one such view, shortfalls of educational achievement
> and attainment . . . are interpreted as deficits of individual effort or will
> . . . These general characterizations ignore differences within groups;
> moreover, they fail to apprehend the qualities of individual lives . . . and
> assign responsibilities for risk in broad measure to the affected groups
> themselves ignoring oppressive and discriminatory conditions. . . .
> (Catterall, 1998: 305, cited in Tilleczek & Ferguson, 2007)

How then does this look in youth research processes? In the example of studying the transition from elementary to secondary school in the Transitions Study (Tilleczek et al., 2009) the research team began with a review of international literature (Tilleczek, 2007b, 2008a) to attend to the range of risk and protective factors and pathways of young people. In producing sampling categories of young people in transition to speak with, the report team examined wider issues of the fit between schools, communities, and the lives of young people rather than simply targeting student habits or academic history.

The report team also examined lived situations of risk/resilience over time in interviews that followed youth over three separate time periods. As Ungar (2008) reminds us, resilience is best understood as the capacity of individuals to *navigate* resources that sustain well-being; the *capacity* of environments to provide resources; and the ability of individuals, their families, and communities to *negotiate* culturally meaningful ways for resources to be shared.

The Trouble with Normal: Social Acts with Friends, Cigarettes, and Cars

In his song 'The Trouble with Normal' Bruce Cockburn illustrates from his uniquely Canadian vantage point that it is wise to consider what is to be thought of as 'normal' in given contexts. Even newer thinking about youth resilience as outlined in the preceding section can invoke a brand of normalcy worth caution. If pathways, trajectories, and resiliency models are the new 'normal', how normal is it for young people to be resilient? How does this work shed light on individuation and identity issues for youth? What are the outstanding problems with this work? Does the suggestion that youth are resilient take us full circle to finding another way to problematize those who are not? Is resilience becoming a further way to attend only to individuals? Will we stop looking for the organization of real troubles and put a mere happy face on young lives? Will we simply continue to look for resilience in a person rather than in the social context?

As was suggested in Chapter 2 of this book, the at-risk labels for youth do continue to permeate investigations of many rites of passage, such as smoking or driving a car. In many cases, adaptation and negotiation of such 'risks' remains tied to individuals, not to the cultures and meanings of schools, friendships, homes, or communities—how can we create resilient institutions? How and to what do these institutions and cultures adapt? The lack of attention to cultural influences continues to limit youth research and practice.

In the case of youth smoking or learning to drive a car, most often cited in contemporary psychological discussions are the 'risk-taking' propensity of youth and 'faulty adolescent cognition'. This literature portrays adolescence as a time of escalating risk-taking that itself results in injury and death (Irwin, 1993; Muuss & Porton, 1998). However, attempts to explain links between risk-taking and such injury have been sparse as compared to the wealth of research aimed at explaining the 'causes' of youth risk-taking behaviour. As stated in Chapter 2, these include a general cognitive incapability (unrealistic self-appraisal and cognitive egocentrism), the inability to perceive risks, and a thrill-seeking personality (Arnett & Balle-Jensen, 1993). It is important to remember that Jelalian et al. (1997) have shown that risk-taking propensity accounts for only 4 per cent of the actual variance in youth injuries. This means that the other 96 per cent of the variability in young people being injured is not explained by risk-taking alone.

More than that, risk is not simply problematic (Tilleczek, 2004; Tilleczek & Hine, 2006) but plays an important part in the positive growth and development of young people. Risk can be seen as an extension of play in childhood and is, in fact, social and transformative for youth (Lightfoot, 1997). Lightfoot's work is akin to Elkind's (1980) classic work. Elkind used social cognitive metaphors to detail Goffman's (1969) notion of strategic interactions and Piaget's (1972) notion of formal operations as jointly used by youth as a negotiation strategy to construct, enhance, and maintain their self-concept. Thus, sneaking out of the house, forging parental signatures to skip school, as well as dating behaviours, forbidden acts of drug use, and phoning behaviours are all related to social and cognitive growth. Such actions have also been shown to become cultural 'edgework' by allowing the very negotiations between self and culture that make for resilience (Lyng, 1993). Thus, contemporary models of youth as individualized problems and deviants who are incompetent, faulty risk-takers require further scrutiny. The extent to which young people view risk-taking as statements about themselves, about who they want to become, or about how they relate to others holds the capacity to be prophylactic against risk (Levitt and Selman, 1996; Lightfoot, 1997). Thus, young people's growing awareness of the character of their own activities within a complex web of social relationships in which they search for rites of passage propels them into the empowered position of adulthood.

Embedded in this argument is the view that traditional risk-taking notions of youth are limited in scope. In addition, attempting to rid youth entirely of these activities negates the social tasks of youth and cultural necessities for identity construction (Lightfoot & Cox, 1997; Gullone et al., 2000). Lightfoot (1997) has suggested ways in which intentional risk-taking happens for a group of American, middle-class youth engaged in less dangerous risky activity, such as sneaking out of the house, drinking, and smoking drugs (for a review, see Keating, 1998). She reports that risk is both social and transformative, taking the place of play and offering opportunity for social developmental growth. Moreover, the meanings and processes of these negotiations and actions require much more scrutiny in youth identity literature. What remains to be studied are the optimal quantity and quality of risk for developmental health, and the ways in which risk is distributed and negotiated in youth culture. Three brief examples will illustrate ways in which youth studies can better attend to these issues.

Can Youth Studies Better Attend to Risk?

Social Integration

The first example of a better approach arises from important work detailing the place of parental and peer relationships in determining the social integration of young people. Social integration, as many have shown, in turn guards against or is protective against negative risk-taking behaviours (Youniss et al., 2001). But Youniss et al. (1997) also suggest important variations in social integration into youth culture such that connection and social integration is associated with self-regulation and adult normative behaviour. Those young people who were more integrated into school norms were also more likely to engage in integrated activities, while those who were less integrated engaged more often in negative health risks. Youniss et al. (1997) suggest the presence of an integrated youth syndrome that is counter to the syndrome of multiple delinquencies.

The more socially central are youth, the less they are likely to self-harm. Conversely, in both Australian (Moore & Parsons, 2000) and Danish populations (Arnett & Balle-Johnson, 1993), the more socially marginalized are youth, the more likely they are to engage in risks that are detrimental. Moreover, these findings correspond to those arising in youth resiliency work such that social integration and self-regulation are protective and supportive even at the level of engagement in health risks. These results can be related to the importance of belonging as a social process, which we have seen in the many cultural nests of youth (schools, communities, with friends, in families, etc.).

Smoking

The second example is related to the first. Smoking is a particular youth health risk that can be examined for its social and cultural meaning and centrality in addition to understanding the negative health consequences. No doubt, the health risks to smokers are real and deleterious in the long term and this line of research is important to work *with* and *for* youth who could perhaps simply quit or refuse to begin smoking. But how is this best accomplished? Population-based studies of youth smoking suggest an ironic element. Youth who smoke have substantial information about the health risks associated with smoking (Ontario Tobacco Research Unit, 1997), state a readiness to quit that decreases after 20 years of age (Stephens & Stephens, 1996), and yet continue to smoke. And despite a growth in prevention and cessation programs for youth, the incidence of experimentation with tobacco has increased steadily over the past 40 years (Addiction Research Foundation, 1998), where nearly 29 per cent of females and 26 per cent of males from ages 12 to 19 years report having smoked in the previous 12 months (Ontario Tobacco Research Unit, 1997). According to the Addiction Research Foundation (1998), over half (55 per cent) of youth smokers have attempted to quit during the previous year and youth smoking remains one of the most consistent predictors of adult smoking (Statistics Canada, 1998).

What accounts for this ironic element of adolescent smoking? The answer is related to the way that smoking begins. Interactive models of smoking (Ward, Klesges, & Halpern, 1997) suggest joint influences of biological and addictive components (withdrawal, weight gain, and craving), cultural components (gender, age, and social context), psychological processes, and demographics (smoking history). However, the interplay of these factors deserves more research attention as it can translate into youth prevention (Pertraitis, Flay, & Miller, 1995). The development of personal meanings of smoking (Levitt & Selman, 1996; Levitt, Selman, & Richmond, 1991) suggests that smoking decisions are bound up with the individual meanings and social identities. As well, such personal meanings of smoking describe an integrative function of knowledge that mediates individual and cultural factors. Assessing the personal meaning of smoking should illustrate the relationships between youth culture and individual smoking acts. Levitt and Selman's (1996) concept of personal meaning has two useful hallmarks for youth studies: the interactive nature of individuals in relation to their culture, and the developmental nature of meaning-making, which is assessed when young people voice their reasons and decisions to smoke.

In integrating these perspectives to study social meanings of smoking, Tilleczek and Hine (2006) designed a study to speak with young people who smoke. From these interviews they found that youth who do know a great deal about the health and social risks of smoking were ready to quit but did not do so. The young people also reported a good deal of inconsistency in the meanings that were made about their smoking. In addition, these interviews showed how age and gender differentiated these meanings. For example, the process of identity and meaning-making were laden with a burgeoning self-reflection on why they continued to smoke, and this self-reflection increased with age and differed by gender. The youngest males (elementary school) in the study cited the fun and thrill of 'holding fire' and the sensual feel of the package, foil, and smoke associated with the act. They also cited peer pressure as one reason they began smoking. The youngest females most often spoke about the need to fit in and to suppress appetite—not unrelated practices in their youth culture.

Among the older youth (high school) a self-reflective knowledge of smoking was expressed such that they saw themselves as part of a growing number of youth who wished to quit but could not. These youth spoke often about addiction as a problem but were reflective of the important place of smoking in their youth culture. One grade 12 male articulated this the following way:

> The thing that I cannot figure out about teenagers is we know the dangers yet we still do it. I can't understand that. I am kind of quitting. . . . Most teenagers have the attitude that nothing can hurt them so I don't think they really care. Maybe I don't have the regular teenage attitude about being invincible because it scares me. (Tilleczek and Hine, 2006: 280)

The study's thematic and developmental analyses revealed differentiation of cultural meaning by age and gender. Discussions of the cultural pros that youth see in smoking are a useful step in intervention, which can empower youth to recognize their smoking patterns and work toward thinking about and negotiating healthier risks to propel their status needs. The youth in this study did hold negative views of smoking and had best friends who were smokers. The fact that they continued to smoke suggests that negative social pressures are enough to create contradiction, but not enough to overcome the addiction and/or need for status. If we recognize that empowerment and status play an important part in youth smoking, prevention could move past the individualistic 'just say no' abstinence approach and look to more heterogeneous and cultural responses.

Driving

A third example of this kind of research is related to another important youth cultural act: driving a car. In the process of learning to drive, young people attain a critical rite of passage into adulthood. However, unlike troubles that occur in other cultural transitions (graduating from high school) becoming a driver can potentially be fraught with expense, injury, or death. In fact, the leading cause of death for young people is injury—most of it due to driving incidents (Tilleczek, in press). Although prevention strategies, such as graduated licensing and driver education, are in place, youth driving injury remains significant. Death by motor vehicle injuries also increases dramatically during this phase of development (Irwin, 1993), a trend that holds steady regardless of whether one examines global (World Health Organization, 1999), national (Health Canada, 1997; Transport Canada, 2001), or provincial trends (Ontario Ministry of Transportation, 2000).

In fact, detailed national data for Canadian youth under 20 years of age show unintentional injuries as the leading cause of death and the second most frequent cause of hospitalization (Health Canada, 1997). In addition, youth is the age group with the highest rates of death and hospitalization for all injury categories in Canada, with males three times more at risk than females. In Canada in 2001, there were 20 million licensed drivers, of whom 1,013,621 were in the 15 to 19 age range (Transport Canada, 2001). Although youth in this age range make up just 6.7 per cent of the total Canadian population, their traffic fatalities and serious injuries account for 63 per cent of all motor vehicle fatalities and serious injuries. In total, youth in the 15 to 19 age range were involved in 29,646 serious injuries and 387 fatalities due to traffic accidents in 2001 (Transport Canada, 2001). Why is this so, and why does it remain so over time? Studies (cf. Tilleczek, 2006) have attempted to answer these questions by investigating and reframing the problem in a cultural context. This approach makes visible the logic and regulation of youth driving culture as it is/is not supportive and preventative.

For example, Csikszentmihalyi and Schneider (2000) have examined the opportunities and constraints of other transitional sites of becoming an adult, such as work, school, and sports. Their results indicate that images of risk and play are embedded in these social experiences. Indeed, it has been shown that young men rate the automobile as providing high levels of enjoyment and satisfaction (Bibby & Posterski, 1996). Firth and Geoffrey (1980, cited in Rothe, 1987) suggest that all youth want to own a car since driving also represents increased social status. The meaning of driving is also related to the ease of getting around and access to culturally appropriate events, such as school/ work-related activities, and is also related to providing freedom (Rothe, 1987). Far from all being 'risky drivers' or individual 'risk-takers' Tilleczek (2006) has shown that young drivers are concerned with safety and wish to go to driver education to become more responsible drivers and citizens. In conducting a critical ethnographic study of youth driving culture, she found age- and gender-related differences in meanings of driving and also reported that drivers' education classrooms were not consistently helpful in addressing the real challenges of driving and more often invoked a demonized notion of young drivers rather than a careful assessment of the real dangers of driving.

Youth driving culture has been mapped out and shown to be illogical and mixed, creating a poor start for the enthusiastic young driver (cf., Tilleczek, 2004; Tilleczek, in press). The classroom practices of driver education have been found to operate as *potential* sources of support for prevention of driving incidents but were not consistently helpful. They are an integral location in the system whereby young drivers access content and curriculum (both hidden and explicit). Within the driver's education setting, competing images of driving exist, illustrating driving as both dangerous and normal. Youth are treated in the classrooms as competent and responsible in preparing to overcome the inherent risks of driving, while the texts and curriculum illustrate youth as an integral part in creating driving dangers. They are also portrayed as taking great risks and demonstrating faulty decision making, but these troubles are seen to be addressed in the class and car instruction. Discussion of the safe and dangerous nature of driving coalesces within certain content, such as becoming a 'defensive driver', 'traffic psychology', and 'handling adverse conditions'. But most often the blame is placed back on 'risky' young people with no clear image of a culture of youth driving. In contrast to the views held by young drivers, the system tends to problematize driving. Youth, on the other hand, see driving as necessary in making their transition to adulthood, as a way to gain independence, and as a means to become mobile. Younger drivers do find driving to be more relaxing, exciting, easy, and less risky than older drivers do (Tilleczek, 2004). However, they are also aware of the dangerous and risky aspects of driving. In fact, they seek driving education to meet the goals and expectations of becoming safe drivers.

Tilleczek (2004) argues that the system's characterization of youth and driving suggests simultaneously normalized and pathologized images. Evidence of a normal, well-regulated, and logically structured driving culture competes with the mixed messages of the dangerous and unregulated nature of driving.

The freedom with which youth access cars and licenses speaks to the view of the 16-year-old as competent enough to handle a machine of this size, albeit with restrictions. The opposing images of extreme danger are also presented in the discourse. The driving culture is therefore portrayed to relate to Beck's (1992) risk society. The danger is pervasive, and the onus of negotiating these risks is placed on the individual, who must 'shop carefully' for a driving school and then apply great caution in learning to drive. This result suggests the further presence of an epistemological fallacy (Furlong & Cartmel, 2007), causing individual blame for danger to persist in a sea of systemic trouble. The trouble takes the forms of system flaws, mixed and ageist messages that do not necessarily reflect youth lives, and lack of coordination within the logic and regulation of driver education. As suggested by Mayhew and Simpson (2002), there is further need for driving education to be integrated and coordinated with secondary schools. The findings of Tilleczek's (2006) study suggest that prevention efforts are based on the assumption (a historical one) that youth are troubled, take risks, and are in need of constant surveillance rather than support. This psychological model places the blame for driving incidents on youth.

However, contested images have been presented both historically and currently that portray youth as a heterogeneous group of active and competent transition makers for whom social location, age, and gender matter (Enright et al., 1987; Griffen, 1997; Marecek, 2002) and who are moving toward resilient environments and behaviours. A move toward unpacking risk has been an important outcome of the study. Risk has been seen to act as a positive strategy in negotiating culture (Lightfoot, 1997; Gullone et al., 2000) and worth rethinking as the key location of prevention in driving. Few novice drivers are interested in risk-taking activities and see the danger of risk-taking while driving. If we are not to blame risky youth for traffic injury, then understanding the regulatory practices and strategies for learning to drive currently in place becomes critical.

Accentuating the Positive

The recent shift in the US and Canada toward the study of 'positive youth development' has emerged from these discussions of risk and resilience. The movement is a turn toward placing the strengths and possibilities of youth at the core of theory and practice by replacing the pathological and negative views that have dominated:

> The current political pastime of 'blaming children' for all social evils is placed in the context of changing national and local agendas. . . . public panics are predictable in that they have little to do with a criminogenic reality but much to do with the economic and political context in which

they arise. Furthermore, crime panics are targeted at vulnerable and marginal people . . . I argue further that the panic that vilifies children is a coordinated, calculated attempt to nourish the ideology that supports a society stratified on the bases of race, class and gender, and that the war on kids is part of the state-business mechanism that continually reproduces an oppressive social and economic order through both labour and consumer exploitation. (Schissel, 1997, pp. 13–14)

Larson (2000) wisely contrasts positive youth development with developmental psychopathology and suggests the former is about 'how things go right' while the latter focuses on 'how things go wrong'. Positive youth development is a line of inquiry regarding 'the pathways whereby children and adolescents become motivated, directed, socially competent, compassionate and psychologically vigorous adults' (Larson, 2000). As Benson and co-authors state, many people have been trying to articulate a clear notion and concept of the field of positive youth development. Their review of these efforts in the *Handbook of Child Psychology* attempts a synthesis of these principles and concepts as follows:

1. All youth have the inherent capacity for positive growth and development.
2. A positive developmental trajectory is enabled when youth are embedded in relationships, contexts, and ecologies that nurture their development.
3. The promotion of positive development is further enabled when youth participate in multiple, nutrient-rich relationships, contexts, and ecologies.
4. All youth benefit from these relationships, contexts, and ecologies. We need support, empowerment, and engaged sets for all youth, generalizing across race, ethnicity, gender, and family income. However, the strategies and tactics for promoting these developmental assets can vary considerably as a function of social location.
5. Community is a viable and critical 'delivery system' for positive youth development.
6. Youth are major actors in their own development and are significant (and underutilized) resources for creating the kinds of relationships, contexts, ecologies, and communities that enable positive youth development. (Benson et al., 2006: 896)

Besides these important guiding principles, those working in this subfield of youth studies tend to coalesce around the ideas of Damon (2004:17) such that 'the positive youth development perspective emphasizes the manifest potentialities rather than the supposed incapacities of young people— including young people from the most disadvantaged backgrounds and those with the most troubled histories'. Definitions tend to focus on some combination of developmental contexts, relationships, the nature of the young person, the active engagement of young people and their strengths, and a set of planned practices and actions to foster positive development and reduce high-risk behaviour. As argued above, however, some high-risk behaviour is itself adaptive and necessary and its meanings require more scrutiny. This of course has implications for those 'planned actions', programs, and policies, which can be more fully informed by cultural meanings. The hypotheses generated from this work and the relations of research to practice and policy will be the content of the final section of the Chapters in the book. The next section of this chapter examines some of these process-related ideas vis-à-vis the potential and possibility of narrative and biography for youth studies.

Biography, Narrative, and Being Revisited

As was stated in Chapter 1 of the book, the social processes of *being, becoming,* and *belonging* can be used as shortcuts to understanding important tensions of the lives and cultures of young people and youth studies. The story is a choice place to examine intersections of being and becoming as surmised from biography, memoir, life history, and other poetic/visual narrative forms:

> Works of literature—plays, some poetry, novels, short stories, films— are based on narrative. As Bruner (1986) has proposed, narrative is that distinctive mode of thought in which we understand human agents, their intentions, and the vicissitudes of these intentions. Bruner might have added that in this mode there is typically also a focus on the emotions that prompt intentions and the emotions that result as these intentions are enacted. (Oatley, 2003: 1)

Such forms of understanding play crucial roles in a social science *with* and *for* youth. As Lawler (2002: 242) asserts, narrative research work in the social sciences fully portray,

> . . . accounts which contain transformation (change over time), some kind of 'action' and characters, all of which are brought together within an overall 'plot'—are a central means with which people connect together past and present, self and other.

Narrative analysis, then, is not only a record of what happened, but 'a continuing interpretation and reinterpretation of our experience . . . it is the best way to understand 'lived time' (Bruner, 2004: 692). It is a specific type of analysis of data used in qualitative research and is useful in that it aids in the exploration of ways that 'social actors interpret the world and their place within it' (Lawler, 2002: 242). There is an ever-growing genre of memoir and biography books and documentary films dedicated to the telling of lives and times of individuals in their social and historical contexts.

The roles of narrative and biography in youth studies are many and varied, from providing ways to speak with young people in research, to providing a space for them to express their experiences and voices, to offering ways to present their lives and work. One role of narrative is as a method for collecting important data, information, and descriptions and providing a space for youth engagement and voice in the research process. Another role is as a process for analyzing the data we collect in qualitative research projects. In opposition to other forms of analysis, such as thematic or discourse analysis, narrative analysis holds lives and experiences in context and attempts to avoid fragmenting or reducing them.

Narrative and biography can also be used as a manner of sharing theoretical or research insights with those parents and practitioners who are at the front line of supporting the lives of young people. The short composite testimonials presented in Chapter 1 are examples of this role. Stories have a great power to move the entire community of people, policy makers and practitioners, toward deeper understanding and action. Finally, narrative and story abound in novels and films about 'coming of age' and the lives of youth. Such works as *Anne of Green Gables*, *The Diary of a Young Girl*, *The Catcher in the Rye*, *Rebel Without a Cause*, *What Is the What: The Autobiography of Valentino Achak Deng*, etc., are just a very few of the myriad tales of youth that continue to be enjoyed and understood as windows into the lives of young people.

Each year across the world (both in schools and outside them), young people themselves write thousands of stories, poems, and post short films or photographs on Facebook or YouTube as a way to tell their stories. Stories are a window into the process of the self and identity within the contexts of social and cultural events and influences. Not just writing stories, but the art of telling them well are of growing interest in youth studies. To demonstrate the contemporary use of story in youth studies is to begin with three short narrative descriptions of young Canadian women with whom one research team has been speaking over the course of three years as they entered into high school (Tilleczek et al., 2009). These narratives have been constructed and written from field notes and interview conversations with young people wherein a research team has used the narrative form of analysis and presentation to make visible the interconnected worlds of young people in transition. Please note that the names used in these narratives are pseudonyms.

All three of these three young women have been in transition from elementary to secondary school, are all the same age, and all reside in the same province of Canada. However, the differences in social supports, regions, social class, and identity process are stark. What else could be surmised about the differences

Box 7.1 Sherry

Sherry lives in a remote community and must travel two hours to school. She lives with a parent, step-parent, and two siblings and mentions her mother as her *biggest support*. Her relationship with one sibling is poor due to extreme bullying, which she endures at home and school. Her parents appear not to be dealing with this situation. Sherry has positive feelings about school and is currently in grade 10, in the applied program. She did fail one core course in grade 9 and is repeating it to recover the credit. Rumours that her sibling had spread impact how school peers treat her, and bullying has extended from her home into the school. She is receiving help in coping from a counsellor and although the school has intervened, such interventions have only temporary results and many have been ineffective, i.e. making her responsible for solving the issue by telling her to ignore bullying. The consequence of this school violence is that she gets angry often and this ruins her concentration and ability to focus on her studies. Sherry feels that she is treated unfairly by some teachers. The long distance between home and school prevents her participation in extracurricular activities after school and nothing offered during school is of interest to her. She was neutral about the transition from elementary to secondary school and was not able to participate in transition events that were hosted by the school since they took place after school and on weekends. Her main advice to those at school would be to give her extra time and help with work to compensate for lost time due to behaviour problems she is experiencing as a result of the constant aggression she deals with at home and school.

Box 7.2 Maya

Maya lives with her single parent and reports good support from her. She also lives with a sibling who has 'given up' academically and their mother has 'given up' on this young person as well. Maya is currently in an academic program and has passed all of her courses so far. She identifies as being different from other students in school due to her minority status as an African Canadian. She was diagnosed with a medical disorder and has

(continued)

Box 7.2 Maya (continued)

always been treated differently by students. She had a 'false start' to her transition when she began high school (grade 9) and found herself to be in risk situations immediately with peers/friends due to skipping school. After a short period of time Maya came to her current high school and remains there. She mentioned that if she becomes confident she will not slide back into 'bad behaviour'. Her mother will let her return to this school if her grades reach A level. She had few friends when she was younger but now is very involved in sports and other clubs and appears to have a good level of social engagement. She reports the curriculum to be weak and scheduling caused initial difficulties with her transition. When she was finally able to start this core course, she was a month behind all the other students. Maya has very positive opinions about teachers and recognizes efforts to help her with her studies, etc. She also recognizes herself as 'talkative' but is trying to change this with help from teachers. She works a few hours over the weekend for one of her teachers doing odd jobs. She appears to have a high involvement in school culture/spirit. She spoke about a career in health care, but also about her long-term interest in music.

Box 7.3 Dakota

Dakota has close ties to her Aboriginal community, family, and friends and notes that her parents are important and protective, socially and academically. She has a sibling in high school and it appears that her sibling and partner are also protective, positive influences for her. In addition, she has another younger sibling for whom she sees herself as a mentor and with whom she reports a very caring, close relationship as well. Dakota takes a long bus ride to and from school each day as she lives in a rural community with only one other public high school. Her only other alternative for school would be to leave her community, which she reports would cause great anxiety. If her family ever moved, she would ask to stay with her grandparent so she could stay at her current school as she believes that going to school with lots of white people would be stressful for her and she wants to stay

> ## Box 7.3 Dakota *(continued)*
>
> in her Aboriginal community. Dakota is neutral about the role of school and transition programs so far, but she does have positive feelings about school. She views her friends as the best feature of high school and has had solid academic and social adjustments. She feels respected and listened to by her friends and wants to be involved in sports in the future. Dakota is not involved in any paid or volunteer work outside of school.

these narratives portray? At present, a conclusion is emerging based upon the kinds of discussions relating to risk and resilience for young people that have been outlined in the preceding sections of this chapter. It appears that these stories and lived experiences of youth can be seen to coalesce around one of three groupings (Tillecek et al., 2010):

1. Young people in mostly risk situations are those with co-occurring, cumulative adversities and intersections at many levels (individual, classroom, home, school, community). For example, they may have had academic difficulties, been highly transient, or placed a low value on school. They may also have experienced negative school cultures (complex *family of schools,* low teacher expectations, etc.) and social risks (racism, poverty, alienation, neighbourhood troubles, and social isolation from friends). These are young people who may have felt that they did not belong, and may also have described multiple reasons.
2. Young people with complex resiliencies are those in obvious risk situations but with real demonstrations for/of potential support and resilience. These are young people who may have been as in category 1 above but who demonstrate evidence of competencies, planning, negotiation, resistance, etc. The young people may have reported such aspects of resilience through their aspirations, academics, and social lives or within schools and communities. Interviews with these young people focus on *how* people and systems can make a difference in their lives rather than on dramatic or heroic narratives (cf. Garmezy, 1991) in which youth overcome all odds on their own.
3. Young people who are mostly protected are those with very little or no apparent risk situations at either cultural or individual levels. They may also demonstrate numerous protective factors and supports in the contexts surrounding them.

How, then, would you characterize Sherry, Maya, and Dakota, and do the brief narrative descriptions provide any depth to their lives? Would simple tables illustrating risk and protective factors suffice to illustrate their individual situations? There is a running debate among narrative researchers about such issues that spans 25 years and is too lengthy to encounter fully in this section. It is sufficient to point out that some researchers are uncovering the problems with overprescribing the methods of narratives. Other researchers are focusing on the processes of counter-narratives and their uses. And there remain those in the field who are still embracing fully the many strands of humanities and social sciences that have entangled to bring us to this moment in narrative forms of knowing:

> We are at an interesting moment in the history of understanding
> imaginative literature. The wars between the post-modernists and
> the traditionalists are almost over. Narratology and cognitive poetics,
> interdisciplinary pursuits both, are on the rise. There is interest in fiction
> within philosophy and psychology, and there is interest in cognition
> among literary theorists. So, for the first time since Aristotle's *Poetics,* we
> may have the chance of an approach to our subject that bridges the arts
> and the sciences. (Oatley, 2003: 1)

This is a tall order but one that has been embraced across disciplines. We can trace the use of narrative forms of knowing from oral storytelling practices of indigenous cultures, from literature, from psychoanalysis, from counselling, etc. Narrative analysis is not only a record of what happened, but a manner in which we interpret and reinterpret being and experience. It is the best way to understand 'lived time' (Bruner, 2004: 692) and to explore the ways that 'social actors interpret the world, and their place within it' (Lawler, 2002: 242). Not only does a narrative reveal much about the teller, but it also gives us insight into the worlds each individual lives in and is influenced by. Moreover, groups of narratives can then be analyzed for similarities and differences while individual narratives are examined for continuities and discontinuities over time.

By using this type of approach and analysis, researchers in youth studies open a window into a better understanding of the lives and stories of young people within many contexts. We may examine the many levels of influence surrounding them (society, community, school, family, and friends) and the fluidity/fixable character of their lives over time. Such crossing over, fluidity, and rigidity of boundaries between these categories are of analytical, practical, and policy interest. Understanding who moves in and out of situations of risk and resiliency and why/how they do so over the course of transitional points is critical. Narrative analyses show both fluidity and rigidity in risk/resiliency across the processes of transition. Risk and protective factors appear, disappear, and reappear for these young people at multiple levels (Tilleczek et al., 2010).

Indeed, the use of narrative and biography in youth studies is opening the field to this kind of understanding and deeper description of the abundance of experience, identity processes, social worlds, and cultures of young people.

Critical Thinking Activities

1. Visit the website of the Learning Partnership's National Dialogue on Resilience in Youth (www.thelearningpartnership.ca/Page.aspx?pid=468). Read the Foundational Document, one of the Provincial Roundtable Reports, and the two additional academic papers (Ungar and Shonert-Reichal). Provide two examples of resilience based on your life as a young person or on the life of another young person you have known. Use Ungar's 'questions to explore' at the end of his article to guide you.

2. Attempt to design a youth-attuned study relating to a different rite of passage in Canadian culture (not smoking or driving or social integration at school). Suggest a way to study this rite of passage and what it may mean to young people.

3. Visit the website of the Centre for Narrative Research in the UK. Use some of the ideas presented in this chapter *and* from the centre to attempt your own analysis of a favourite 'coming of age' or youth-related film.

Further Readings

Bruner, J. (1986). *Actual Minds, Possible Worlds*. Cambridge: Harvard University Press.

Erikson, E.H. (1958). *Young Man Luther: A Study in Psychoanalysis and History*. New York: W.W. Norton.

Suggested Websites

The Centre for Narrative Research
www.uel.ac.uk/cnr/index.htm

Learning Partnership—National Dialogue on Resilience in Youth
www.thelearningpartnership.ca/Page.aspx?pid=468

Chapter Eight

Action, Practice, and Policy *with* and *for* Youth

The health and social problems which we have found to be related to inequality tend to be treated by policy makers as it they were quite separate from one another, each needing separate services and remedies. We pay doctors and nurses to treat ill-health, police and prisons to deal with crime, remedial teachers and educational psychologists to tackle educational problems and social workers, drug rehabilitation units, psychiatric services and health promotion experts to deal with a host of other problems. These services are all expensive and none of them is more than partially effective. For instance, differences in the quality of medical care have less effect on people's life expectancy than social differences in their risks of getting some life-threatening disease in the first place. And even when the various services are successful in stopping someone re-offending, in curing cancer, getting someone off drugs, or dealing with educational failure, we know that our societies are endlessly recreating these problems in each new generation. Meanwhile, all these problems are most common in the most deprived areas of our society and many times more common in more unequal societies. (Wilkinson & Pickett, 2009)

Whilst many texts related to youth and the 'problems' posed by particular groups of young people would be prefaced with rationales concerning the moral panics of the day, relatively few analyses have posed the question 'why is there so much research and/or policy-related interest in young people?' or 'why does youth research take particular forms in given historical and political contexts?' (Griffen, 1997)

Introduction

This chapter outlines ways in which people work *with* and *for* young people. Chapters 3 and 4 showed how this work often includes research but how programs and policies are ill-informed by it. Some research is more rigorous and better than others at including, listening to, and hearing youth. Other youth work includes the creation of programs thought to assist in a variety of ways, for example, community-based youth centres, programs to help young offenders, driving lessons for young people, etc. In addition, there are policies and laws enacted to govern young people and the institutions and programs that are established. For instance, each high school in Canada is governed by a set of laws (education acts) and policies originating in the provincial government's education ministry and in turn enacted by boards of education, by schools, by administrators, and by educators. But how many of these programs, practices, and policies are well-informed by solid youth-attuned research? How much research is informed by the programs, policies, and social actions of youth?

Youth-driven social actions are often either overlooked or undervalued. Young people themselves create and maintain their own groupings, programs, activities, and social movements. As Feixa et al. (2009) describe, the 'new, new social movements' of youth are anti-corporate, dynamic, transnational, and intergenerational, and make use of technologies to agitate in relation to local identities and global modernity. Youth social actions may work against regulations and existing programs or policies (local, transnational, global) that attempt to govern them. They act directly to 'jam the culture' or to either engage in or resist modern social, economic, and political forces. Young people also act indirectly through the formal channels to make the changes they feel are necessary. In each case, youth are publicly, civically, and socially active and engaged. So, too, are those who run programs, write policy, enact laws, and govern social institutions for young people. Young people are treated in relation to the ideas that exist about them at any given time. In this way, the complex cultural nests of youth can be witnessed by observing the state and quality of youth services, programs, institutions, and policies. And we are urged to ask, why these social programs and actions? Why now?

This final chapter of the book provides examples of each kind of action *with*, *for*, and *by* young people. It also binds the threads that run through the book to conclude about the state of youth studies as seen in policy, practice, and action. How could youth studies further our work for young people? How can our best evidence uncover and inform youth social action, programs, and practices? To what end will this occur?

Youth Studies as Youth Practice: A Reflexive Relationship

There are many ways to generate information, observations, and understandings about youth. The main ideas arising in Chapters 3 and 4 were to perform research as praxis through forms of critical social inquiry designed specifically with young people in mind. For instance, the effectiveness of art-based, biographical, and narrative tools was discussed to allow for the exploration of both identity/experience and the social organization/reproduction that are important to understanding contemporary youth. It was further suggested that notions of *liminality* and tensions in the social processes of *being*, *becoming*, and *belonging* should be examined. And, at the same time, the cultures that surround and organize these processes for youth are to be studied. The complex cultural nesting approach points to work with a focus on the meso-level of these cultural nests wherein the processes of identity, culture, and modernity intersect and can be clearly observed.

Research *with* and *for* young people must leave young people in a better condition than they were found. It should be also be research *by* youth. This can be accomplished by engaging them in the process, by developing research designs intended to enhance their thinking, by leaving them with knowledge and skills that they had not yet acquired, and by providing a space for their education and experience, in Dewey's sense of the term. The specific suggestions and aims of such research arising from Chapters 3 and 4 were as follows:

- To attend to youth-attuned research through the use of critical strategies
- To attend to an action and social justice orientation *with*, *for*, and *by* young people
- To attend to level and scope of experience, social structures, social processes, and praxis
- To attend to sameness, difference, diversity, and inequality in the study of youth
- To attend to social history and the representations/treatment of youth
- To animate conversations with those invested (and especially with those who are not!)

But how do we converse with others about what we jointly come to know about the lives and times of youth? Once generated, what happens to this knowledge? Will it (can it?) make a difference? Do teachers come to know the best research evidence that can assist in meeting the needs of students? Do physicians and public health personnel come to know the work of mental health researchers on youth depression and anxiety? Is the research *with*, *for*, and *by* young people sufficiently grounded in their lived experiences and cultural nests?

In a recent article on methodological considerations of youth research, evidence-based practice is discussed as a potential way to provide solutions to problems that arise (Mueller, Tilleczek, et al., 2008). Evidence-based practice is a systematic application of rigorously observed knowledge. But Mueller et al. (2008) discuss a more reflexive approach that acknowledges why scientific facts cannot be so applied. Real-life problems are complex and cannot be solved by deducing steps. Given that theories and research do not provide a recipe for 'fixing' problems, a reflective approach to evidence-based practice assigns both practitioners (educators, health personnel, parents, youth justice personnel, etc.) and young people more central roles. In interacting with knowledge and facts, practitioners integrate the best evidence possible and make practical decisions for their work with young people. Research evidence is only one part of it; the professional experience of the person working with youth *and* the observations and actions of young people need also to be considered. Practitioners also have the responsibility to integrate the cultural values and ethical issues of young people into their decision process. This has consequences for professional practice and for future research.

There are some good examples of reflexive evidence-based work in Canada. In working across the range of cultural nests of young people, the Community Health Systems Resource Group (CHSRG) of the Hospital for Sick Children in Toronto:

> works to increase community capacity and to improve outcomes for children, youth and families through research and community partnerships. Comprised of a group of dedicated health-systems research scientists, the CHSRG coordinates research and provides outreach to improve the well-being and mental health of children. The CHSRG works to promote success in children and youth by considering all factors essential to well-being including health, home life, school, community life, and peer relationships. The CHSRG advocates for the implementation of evidence-based interventions and standardized outcome measurement in health, mental health, social services and education, and the promotion and facilitation of integration and collaboration in service delivery. The CHSRG uses these links to create 'communities of practice' around pathways and barriers to accessing services and in implementing evidence-based practices. In addition, CHSRG scientists use their research as 'natural laboratories' in knowledge transfer and implementation of practice change by organizing resources to investigate and improve transfer and uptake of innovations in practice. (CHSRG website, January 2010)

The goals of the CHSRG are to:

> improve services for children and youth at the community level; build community commitment to children and youth; and advocate for strong policies at all levels of government that support children, youth and their families. This group of researchers works to share 'research and policy analysis skills, as well as our knowledge of programs and interventions with community leaders, service agencies, and governments who, in turn, share their knowledge and expertise with us. We build and develop partnerships between different community sectors so that priorities, policies, and interventions are jointly planned, implemented, and disseminated.' (CHSRG website, January 2010)

The links between sound research, sharing this work, and joint advocacy for youth are clear. The next section illustrates one such kind of advocacy mechanism in the arena of social policy. The subsequent section will examine more direct action that starts with young people themselves. Significantly, in some policy and governmental arenas, the will to include the 'voices' of youth can be detected. Questions remain about whose voices are included, what actually gets heard and why, and what difference it makes to the everyday lives of young people who are the most marginalized.

Social Policy *with* and *for* Youth

One concrete example of the kind of reflective evidence-based process discussed in the previous section comes from an international school-based mental health consortium. This consortium includes many leading researchers in Canada and abroad who wish to close the support gaps that their work has demonstrated to exist for young people with mental health issues. The wisdom of broaching these gaps within and across schools has been affirmed since young people spend a good deal of their time in public schools and since the outcomes of their education have such a profound impact on their lives. In order to systematically study effective means by which we can begin to create school-based mental health programming and practices, the group conducted a large-scale review of the literature for lessons learned from around the world. A report was produced outlining these lessons, but a policy-oriented report was also written with an executive summary for each of policy makers, practitioners, and researchers (Santor, Short, & Ferguson, 2009). The commitment to attempt to share and use the new knowledge *with* and *for* young people at multiple levels is demonstrated.

For example, the policy implications were given after a consultation across ministries that govern the practices for youth (for example, the Ministries of Education, Health, Children and Youth Services, Citizenship and Immigration). After reviewing these policies and practices and the international literature, the research team suggested that they a) establish an inter-ministerial body to address mental health, b) use evidence-based programs and train practitioners in them, c) research and practise collaboration at the community level, and d) use ongoing research to produce sound evidence at the provincial level (Santor, Short, & Ferguson, 2009).

This kind of policy-setting process also happens at the international and global levels. The United Nations Convention on the Rights of the Child (CRC) was adopted by the UN General Assembly in 1989 and has now been ratified by many individual countries, including Canada. There is no intended hierarchy of rights in the CRC but they include the right to life, the right to survival, the right to develop to the fullest capacity, protection against discrimination of all kinds, the right to live in a safe and healthy environment, the right to expression, and the right to participate fully in family, cultural, and social life. As a set of interrelated statements about the rights of young people, the CRC is the first legally binding global policy to incorporate both civil and political rights with economic, social, and cultural rights. Of course, there are gaps between what countries ought to do for youth and what is actually happening in each country. Indeed, the UN states that 'no single country could yet claim that they honour or protect all of the rights as outlined in the CRC' (UN Website, 2010). But a perusal of the United Nations website illustrates the offshoots of the CRC in myriad programs and policies for youth that have emerged since ratification.

In summary, social policy has been conceived of in many ways. Recently, a Canadian researcher has suggested that policy should be the intersection of prevention, intervention, and innovation by way of state tools that are put into place via money, information, and legislation/documentation about societal ideals (Willms, 2009). In imagining a policy framework for Canada's children and youth based on his work in analyzing the National Longitudinal Survey of Children and Youth, Willms (2009) goes on to suggest government levels of responsibility in reducing vulnerabilities that compromise the well-being of young people. He suggests a five-point plan: (1) delivering good services, especially for those needing support; (2) monitoring and reporting trends and data; (3) drafting and enacting protective legislation; (4) supporting research and practice innovations in these areas; and (5) overseeing capacity-building in families, schools, and communities.

Of course, these acts are neither mutually exclusive nor are they exhaustive of the work that is required. Social policy can simply be used to rationalize political decisions and actions (think of apartheid in South Africa). Moreover, there are problems with human rights discourses as they do not always govern real practice, and they focus on the individual level rather than communities and families or the social organization of the root of problems for youth. Moreover, they may overlook the work that young people are themselves doing when they are excluded from governmental, legal, and policy conversations.

Social Action *with*, *for*, and *by* Youth

A fitting way to conclude the book is with an examination of the social actions of youth as they themselves agitate and negotiate their identities in modern society. Youth social movements are conceptualized in historical and social contexts in keeping with the themes of this book:

> The rise of the 'old' social movements in the nineteenth century was
> connected to the emergence of industrial society, often perceived
> as masculine, adult and class-based struggles, even if many of the

protagonists were actually students, bohemians and young workers, giving rise to a new social actor: the *adolescent* (based on the 'Tarzan' syndrome: the youngster who tries to become an adult). The rise of the 'new' social movements in the 1960s was connected to the emergence of new modes of collective action in the era of mass media and youth countercultures. These were often multi-class and multi-gendered youth struggles, giving rise to another new social actor: the extended adolescent (based on the 'Peter Pan' syndrome—the youngster who refuses to became an adult). The rise of the 'new new' social movements in the 2000s is connected to the emergence of new modes of collective activism in an era of global networks and youth cybercultures: intergenerational, trans-sexual and cross-class struggles, giving rise to yet another new social actor: the 'yo yo' *adultescent* (based on the 'Replicant' syndrome—the youngster who is in between Blade Runner conservatism and android resistance). (Feixa, Pereira, & Juris, 2009: 423)

Feixa et al. (2009) provide a concise history of youth action in the anti-corporate globalization movement, one way in which youth engage in direct action. Using examples from European cities, such as Lisbon and Barcelona, the authors cite a good deal of literature on youth movements that outline the unique characteristics of 'new, new social movements,' which include:

(i) an emphasis on globalism and transnationality and their articulation with local contexts; (ii) the use of new information and communication technologies, particularly the Internet; (iii) the articulation of economic and identity based demands; (iv) the development of innovative forms of action; (v) the creation of new forms of organization; and (vi) the gathering of diverse traditions and organizations under a common umbrella. (Feixa et al., 2009: 425)

With this list of characteristics in place, it is reasonable to ask the following questions: What are contemporary youth up against? To what are they acting and reacting? What do they value and feel to be of social importance?

Canadian youth are said to be most concerned about crime, the economy (poverty), racial discrimination, drugs, violence, the environment, political unity, and the US influence on Canada (Bibby, 2001). Nearly three-quarters (74 per cent) of Canadian youth stated that they support gay rights and 71 per cent feel that the Young Offenders Act should be toughened. As well, honesty and humour were the most important interpersonal values cited by Canadian youth (Bibby, 2001). Canadian youth also highly value friendship and freedom, followed by success and comfort in life. They also value acts of concern for others and a good family life (Bibby, 2001).

In addition, issues of social comparison are important for young people such that four in ten stated that their looks are 'very important' to them and being recognized and valued by a group of friends is more important than having power or popularity in a general sense. These trends have also been reported by others who show that the *perception* of social class (feeling as though you have more money in comparison to other young people) is related to feelings of belonging more than is *actual* family income (Tilleczek et al., 2010). New evidence is also showing that such feelings as having *relatively* less status and money, fewer friends, etc. (the mechanisms of social comparison) are the drivers through which social inequalities in society are manifest as health and social problems (Wilkinson & Pickett, 2009). It is this set of social relations that reproduces inequalities at the level of homes, communities, classrooms, schools, etc.

If young people feel relatively less socially valued by virtue of age, ethnicity, region, social class, gender, etc., what then do they do to negotiate, engage in, and/ or resist the social relations that surround them? All actions young people take to engage in or resist modern society are neither praiseworthy nor problematic. We observe a whole range of human responses in the social actions of youth. However, these actions happen within their own social milieu on a daily basis and are aimed at the larger societal and/or smaller school or community levels. Some more recent and compelling examples include actions that are taken against the prevailing issues discussed in this book, for example, commodification and consumer culture issues (Chapter 5), critical responses to contemporary schools (Chapter 6), global engagement in environmental and social issues (Chapter 4), and enactment of the positive values of commitment, honour, and honesty of young people (Chapter 7). Following, a few examples are provided of each.

Jamming the Modern Culture with Direct Social Action

Upon the publication of Naomi Klein's (2000) book *No Logo: Taking Aim at the Brand Bullies*, and of Kalle Lasn's (1999) book *Culture Jam: How to Reverse America's Suicidal Consumer Binge—And Why We Must*, there was popular excitement about the idea that people (especially young people) could fight against the growth of commodities in society. Klein and Lasn and other authors argued that we need to think about what we buy and about the amounts we consume and proposed the idea 'jamming the culture' or working against (resisting) mass consumerist lifestyles. While the idea of culture jamming was not necessarily new, it gained momentum for young people. The following description (from an *Adbusters* article—the magazine created by Kalle Lasn) attempts to describe culture jamming:

> The term 'culture jamming' has been around a while. Negativland
> coined it on their *Jamcon* '84 (SST) cassette, referring to billboard
> alteration and other forms of media sabotage: 'As awareness of how the
> media environment we occupy affects and directs our inner life grows,
> some resist . . . The skillfully reworked billboard . . . directs the public

viewer to a consideration of the original corporate strategy. The studio for the cultural jammer is the world at large.' Negativland, then, took an active role in conducting media pranks . . . the term was adopted and used by other media activists in the line of work. *Open Magazine Pamphlet Series* spotlighted culture jamming in its July 1993 issue. Tracing it back to Negativland, writer Mark Dery surveyed the varied forms it has taken in media activism: hoaxing, audio agitprop, billboard banditry, guerilla semiotics, zines, etc. Dery makes it quite obvious that *Adbusters'* 'subvertising' is but one take on culture jamming. Realizing Negativland's view of the world-as-studio, Dery places the creative process at the heart of culture jamming. But *Adbusters* has its own ideas about culture jamming. . . . [W]hat comes out is no real alternative to our culture of consumption. Just a different brand. (retrieved January 2010 from www.stayfreemagazine.org/9/adbusters.htm)

In *Culture Jamming: Confronting the Capitalist Colonization of Social Space* (Bowes, 2004), Bowes undertakes an ethnographic study to look at youth political activism and the place of culture jamming in it. He attends demonstrations and speaks to young people who are engaged in culture jamming to find out what it means to them and how their work is socially organized. In the process, he uncovers a critical and rich way to describe culture jamming that moves beyond more journalistic accounts. He argues that,

[t]here is a severe disjuncture that exists between how culture jamming is portrayed in society by the police, mass media, and the actual people who engage in these practices. Many people with whom I have engaged in culture jamming or know to have practiced culture jamming, seem to always connect their work to a deeper political meaning. I can remember numerous discussions I have had . . . connecting it to a broader political framework. On the other hand, mass media reports on culture jamming seem to draw different conclusions. The broader mainstream media generally seem to report culture jamming as senseless work, vandalism, or violence towards private property. Further adding to this social conceptualization, culture jamming is generally portrayed as some form of youth social deviance. This perception of youth social deviance, as Bernard Schissel suggests, is a coordinated and calculated attempt to nourish the ideology that supports a society stratified on the bases of race, class, and gender, and the war on [youth]. (Bowes, 2004: 1–2)

The interesting point about acts of culture jamming is that they signal the elements of modern cultures against which young people are resisting. The culture of consumption, turning all things into commodities, making fetishes out of material things, and losing power and status due to age are a few critical elements that reverberate in other forms of youth action. And this kind of direct action in moments of collective civil disobedience, protest, and demonstration are important in providing clues to what young people are up against and what they are prepared to do in resistance. The direct action of the 'new, new' social movements are well mapped out by Feixa et al. (2009). They trace the 1999 Seattle, US, protest against the World Trade Organization as the first mass protest (approximately 50,000 people) of the new anti-globalization movement, to examples from Brazil, Mumbai, Nairobi, Genoa, Barcelona, and Lisbon. Providing a social and economic history of social action from early Paris communes to these contemporary examples, Feixa et al. (2007) argue for the centrality of young people. In modernity's anti-corporate globalization movements,

> [o]ne of the major characteristics of the 'new, new' social movements is precisely the interaction between different generations of collective action as well as different generations of individual activists. Concrete and universal demands, traditional and innovative action repertoires, old issues and new proposals are aligned under common umbrellas in a multidimensional, fractal way. 'Old', 'new' and 'new, new' social movement demands are interrelated, as are their forms of action. Strictly social questions are interspersed with more cultural and symbolic issues. Indeed, youth subcultures and counter-cultural forms exist in relation to political and economic concerns. In this sense, if new social movements were conceived as identity-based movements, 'new, new' social movements combine cultural and material demands, as well as local and global scales of action. (Feixa et al., 2009: 438)

The 1950s and 1960s civil rights movement in the US provides another example of young people taking direct social action to secure freedoms for their families and communities. These young people rallied against racism, terror, and deeply entrenched social inequalities as seen in violent acts such as the torture and murder of 14-year-old Emmett Till for speaking to a white woman in Mississippi. And young people reacted to the Alabama church bombing in 1957 that killed four young black girls. With the backdrop of racism and segregation extending back generations in their communities, these young people endured beatings, arrests, and death, and commented on the joys of social action and change. Levine (1993) provides narrative and biographical accounts of 'freedom's children' in telling the stories of young civil rights activists. Her collection of experiences and contexts capture the work of these youth and their place in the history of the civil rights movement: 'Read together, they are a patchwork of meanness, bigotry, anger, humour, pain, hope and most of all, courage' (Levine, 1993: 2). The photographs and stories are powerful historical records of these social actions and experiences of young people. Two of these stories are presented in the next text boxes.

Box 8.1 Ricky Shuttlesworth

In 1957 I was starting the ninth grade and supposed to go to Parker, an all-black high school. Phillips was all-white. Where I lived, you'd have to go past Phillips to get to Parker. It didn't make sense. Phillips had much more to offer. At Parker we didn't have the equipment or the facilities. I knew Phillips was a better school. So we decided to enroll. It was an effort to break down segregation. Daddy said, 'You're going,' and I trusted his judgement. I never really showed fear because I was always taught to be strong. Being a 'PK', a preacher's kid, you couldn't always let your feelings show. A lot of time I had played out a scenario in my mind. But it was so frightening that sometimes you didn't deal with it. You just did it. I'm sure I was nervous the day we went, but then again I was with my father and that alleviated some of the nervousness.

I didn't expect the mob that was there. It's not that I expected a positive reception either. They hadn't been positive for the other things we did, like the bus rides or the sit-ins. But even before we pulled up, when we turned up the street, we saw this tremendous number of people. All whites. Everywhere. I don't remember any of the dialogue that went on. I just thought, 'Are we going in there?'

I could not believe that Daddy got out of the car. The crowd started to beat him. Mother got out. Then I started to get out of the car to get my mother and my father and somebody slammed the door on my right ankle. There was mass confusion, but I have blanked it out of my mind. My sister and I have never talked about what happened that day.

Somehow we were all in the back of the car. Reverend Phifer was with us that day. I remember Daddy saying, 'Don't run the stop sign.' We went to the hospital. Daddy was on the stretcher and he wanted to know if everybody was okay. We sat in the hall for a little while, waiting. I didn't know what was happening, if Daddy was okay. He was so broken down, shallow breathing and I thought he was dying. I couldn't believe that people would hurt him like that. They beat him with chains and stuff. I was just in shock that they were so vicious.

Somebody said we did it in the name of freedom. What my sister said stuck in my mind. If she had to go back in that crowd again, she said she would have a fork as a weapon. But, we are nonviolent, and as I think about it, what good would a fork do?

We discovered at the hospital that my mother had been stabbed. That was even more upsetting. She was stabbed in the hip, and I wasn't aware of it. She never let us know how she was hurt or how she was suffering.

Source: Levine, 1993: 44.

Box 8.2 Barbara Howard

I was one of the first to integrate a movie theatre. I remember that evening. The MIA put us in pairs, two to the Paramount and two to the Empire theatre. I integrated the Empire theatre. They did not let us in the first time we tried. We went back a week later, and then they let us in. I remember sitting in the centre aisle, scared to death. Fortunately, there were not many whites there. I remember that distinctly. But boy, we did not stay for the entire movie—I remember that much too. It was the symbolic entering, integration, of the place. I was so scared; I don't remember what the movie was.

What if an older redneck did something to us, then how would we respond? We had been taught if you had to speak, let it be something polite. No cursing. If they struck you, we were told how to crouch and protect ourselves. No fighting back. Would I be able to do what we were taught? That was the fear.

Source: Levine, 1993: 80.

Levine recounts how the civil rights movement in the US was often based on nonviolent protest at many levels. Student sit-ins and protests escalated in the 1960s when four young black college students in North Carolina sat at a 'white' lunch counter at a Woolworth's store. They remained seated and were not served. But their protest action spread to demonstrations, marches, and sit-ins so that 'by 1965 scarcely a day went by without a nonviolent protest in some southern city or town' (Levine, 1993: 74). Even young people in the eighth and ninth grades became very involved.

Indirect Social Actions

This kind of courageous direct and nonviolent social action was modelled for these young civil rights activists. They were supported and encouraged to be a part of a political and social justice movement of major significance. In

> ### Box 8.3 Craig and Marc Kielburger
>
> Craig and Marc Kielburger have had an incredible journey toward the founding of Free the Children and their more recent youth-oriented Me to We program. A quick search of their websites (see List of Suggested Websites on page 143) shows the depth and breadth of the commitments of thousands of young people to social justice around the world. At the level of local communities, young people host numerous events for raising funds and awareness of the plight of less privileged youth around the world. Indeed, these thousands of young people also act on their commitments with a host of actions in other countries. What does this tell us about the potential for youth to enact change?

contemporary Canadian society, some adults view the exclusion of young people in their social, political, and civic education and action to be worthy of real concern. At the very time that young people are suspended in prolonged and commodified youth cultures, alarm bells around their failing civic and political education are ringing. Many young people and adults alike are working in more indirect ways to make spaces for engagement in political and social analysis and for action, which are required for full membership in democratic society.

For instance, the Extreme Kindness Tour by four British Columbia youth and Craig and Marc Kielburger's Me to We Foundation (with Free the Children as an integral part) are 'social enterprises' that strive to get young people positively involved in local and global social justice work. In both cases, the upbeat and positive images of young people form the cornerstone of the projects while the young people responsible for forming these groups work toward youth inclusion and empowerment in political and social action. The idea of global and local understanding and action is at the heart of their message to young people. Most interesting is to see the number of young people who have engaged in this form of social justice action when given the invitation and space to do so.

For instance, there is a recent focus by the Canadian Education Association (CEA) on a youth agenda that directly attempts to discuss issues of marginalization and inclusion of contemporary Canadian young people. The goal is to understand how young people consider their futures and the place that education plays in them. The CEA has endeavoured to find ways to include more and more young people in decision making and in discussions on matters relating to school and education. The CEA is not only reaching out to hear young people's views on public education and to engage them in debate, it is trying to act on what it hears in a variety of ways. See Box 8.4 for a quotation from the association's *Agenda for Youth* (2007).

Box 8.4 Why Youth?

'Respect us', 'Don't judge us', 'Teach us', 'We want to succeed', 'Teachers make all the difference'—These were the messages that 27 students from Halifax, Toronto, and Vancouver sent to educators through the drama *Imagine a School . . .* , a provocative kick-off to CEA's national conversation: *Getting It Right for Adolescent Learners*. Available on DVD, Imagine a School . . . has been seen and discussed by well over 6,000 educators in Canada and the United States. As a follow up to this initiative, twenty students from Riverside School Board joined us in Montreal to create *Designs for Learning Spaces, Learning Relationships and Learning Programs*. Through these powerful experiences, it became clear that we owe it to each of these students and to their peers across Canada to act on all that we have learned from them.

Why Now?

Youth is not primarily a biological phenomenon; it is a social construct. Our ideas about who young people are in relation to society change over time. The impacts of globalization, technological developments, immigration and migration have an especially direct impact on youth. The movement of manufacturing jobs to low wage economies and the growth of high-skilled jobs have eliminated 'softlandings' for young people who do not graduate from high school. Post-secondary education in university or college including apprenticeships is a minimal basis from which young people can develop sustainable livelihoods. Young people are constructing their identities in a pluralistic society of great complexity—aboriginal heritage, affiliations to countries and cultures of origin, gender and sexual orientation, disability and non-disability, and the different aspirations and expectations of young people in urban and rural communities.

Source: CEA Agenda for Youth, 2007: 1.

Critical Thinking Activities

1. Find three short digital stories about young people who are actively engaged in some form of social action. What are they doing and why are they doing it? In each case, make an assessment as to whether or not you feel that this social action could actually making a difference in the lives of modern young people. Why/why not?

2. Read the UN Convention on the Rights of the Child. Which articles do you feel are the most important for addressing the problems and challenges of contemporary youth? Explain.

Further Readings

Feixa, C., Pereira, I., & Juris, J. (2009). Global citizenship and the 'New, New' social movements: Iberian connections. *Young*, 17: 421.

Santor, D., Short, K., & Ferguson, B. (2009). *Taking mental health to school: A policy-oriented paper on school-based mental health for Ontario*. Ottawa: Provincial Centre for Excellence in Child and Youth Mental Health.

Woodhead, M. (2001). Psychology and the construction of children's needs. In A. Prout & A. James (Eds), *Constructing and reconstructing childhood* (pp. 63–84). London: RoutledgeFalmer.

Suggested Websites

Extreme Kindness
http://extremekindness.com/

Free the Children
www.freethechildren.com/

Me to We
www.metowe.com/

United Nations Educational Materials
http://cyberschoolbus.un.org/

Conclusion

The statements ending Chapter 8 about the modern realities in which young people live and about our understandings of youth are in line with many of the ideas presented in this book. Throughout this text I have examined the impacts of technology and globalization and the fundamental social processes of *being*, *becoming*, and *belonging* that are critical to the development of young people. While it is heartening to see that some groups and agencies are beginning to reflect and act on emerging youth studies, this not enough given the ongoing inequalities and marginalization of too many young people, their heightened experiences of depression or anxiety, their dissatisfaction with public schooling, their health struggles and their pleas for a better education.

This book has begun to point out places and processes for continuing work *with*, *for*, and *by* young people. It presents a set of reflective propositions for debate and discussion as we move this work ahead. These eleven propositions form an end to the book. But they also invite readers into an ongoing debate and critical discussion as to their use for young people and for youth studies.

1. *There is real value in rigorous study of young people.* The way in which they are actively negotiating their social lives, and not just how adults have constructed life for them, is critical to the study of youth yet is an aspect of youth studies that is often ignored. The International Sociological Association's XVII World Congress of Sociology has hosted discussions relating to what counts as rigorous research in youth studies. This book suggests that this relates to our theories and questions about young people and the processes of inquiry we use to examine them.

2. *Young people and the study of youth have varied across cultural and historical contexts.* There are both continuities and discontinuities: biological immaturity and growth are continuous, but not necessarily the meanings, models, and methods of youth study or the ways that young people are treated or act. More cross-cultural and historical work is required in youth studies. In addition, we need to attend to the actual everyday treatment of young people and their actions, responses, and resistances.

3. *Complex cultural nests hold the experiences, structures, and timing of continuities and discontinuities of youth.* Youth studies cannot be separated from the lived experiences, social organization, and reproduction of age, ethnicity, social class, race, region, sexualities, gender, and their intersections. Processes of marginalization require further exploration in the institutions that hold and govern young people.

4. *The epistemological fallacy of modern society tends to obscure such analyses* by attending to individual issues and problems that are in fact organized in larger social, political, economic, and cultural processes and structures.

5. *Complex cultural nests take into consideration the intersections of social class, age, race, region, ethnicity, sexuality, and gender at multiple levels of systems while focusing on the daily experiences of young people as lived at the meso level.* The meso level is the liminal and in-between zone where we can best observe the embodiment, interaction, and coming together of social and cultural systems. Complex cultural nests surround the daily social processes of *being, becoming,* and *belonging,* which are so critical to young people.

6. Being *is a fundamental social process that reminds us to observe and value the everyday life experiences of young people.* Young people can be taken at their word, and examined and valued for who they are now. It is also critical to examine identity processes and individualization at the heart of *being.* Communities of beings surround young people at each level and create or negate the belonging that is critical to them.

7. Becoming *is a fundamental social process that reminds us that young people and youth studies are also shifting and in flux across time.* These shifts are conceptualized as nested transitions that are being made from childhood to adulthood and negotiated in many social institutions and settings. Flexible, complex, nuanced trajectories and pathways are the channels by which we witness *becoming.*

8. Belonging *is a fundamental social process having to do with fitting in, finding one's sense of place, and feeling some sense of integration* into the social worlds that are important to young people. Friendships, peer groups, community activities, and civic and political engagement are some of the ways in which belonging is enacted.

9. *Transitions have often been mistakenly conceptualized to be simple, linear, and leading to a specific kind of 'successful' end point* as defined by the state, government officials, parents, or educators. Young people should be asked to articulate their own goals and dreams. Transitions are in fact nested, complex, and *non*-linear, which can be seen in the stories and biographies of youth as they intersect with the cultures and structures they negotiate. Transitional points in the lives of young people are important locations of study, and their meanings and processes require further elaboration.

10. *Research and practice are often separated and targeted at only one or another level of analysis* without seeing the social organization, interconnections, cultural nests, or nested transitions young people negotiate. Reflective evidence-based practices are required to inform the programs and policies addressing young people. Moreover, the direct and indirect actions of young people are an important and often overlooked source of social justice engagement.

11. *The main preoccupations of youth studies are culture, development, and praxis.* Each of these ideas is contested and requires serious discussion, scholarship, and debate. Those working *with* and *for* young people must

make plain their usage of these and other preoccupations which embed their assumptions about the social worlds of youth. This set of reflective propositions has been set out in the book within the context of these social worlds, lives, and times of young people. The book has also discussed the ways in which youth have been studied and understood and has demonstrated the many ways in which the field of youth studies is in flux. In so doing, the book has invited readers into an ongoing conversation about what it is to study and live with young people and how best to do it. This has been shown to be less straightforward a task than often imagined.

The selections of research and practice examples have illustrated the paradox of youth studies. There are clear moments of success, social action, and negotiations of forward-thinking policy and practice. However, the challenges and successes of youth are also made plain as we dig a little and come to better understand their lives and times. The positive news is that there are many scholars who are considering the critical nuances of emerging social theory and methods to assist in detailing the range of possibilities and problems of living as a young person. However, those who work with or govern young people must become better informed about the emergence of this work and be open to the stories and voices of young people.

As such, the book is a cautiously optimistic view of young people and the field of youth studies. It asks those of us who work with and for young people to continue to produce evidence and theory across disciplines in answering questions and examining contexts and to ground an emerging youth studies in the roots of experiences, social justice, and discussions about a good society. Young people are one of the most critical divining rods of modern society. As such, our work in understanding their lives and times reflects the manners of all of us.

Bibliography

Addiction Research Foundation. (1998). Ontario secondary school drug use survey. Toronto: Addiction Research Foundation.

Adlaf, E ., Paglia, A., Ivis, F., & Ialomiteneau, A. (2000). Nonmedical drug use among adolescent students: Highlights from the 1999 Ontario Student Drug Use Survey. *Canadian Medical Association Journal, 162,* 1677–1680.

Alexander, L. (2007). They should make it more normal: Young people's critical standpoints and the social organization of sexuality education. Unpublished Master's Thesis: Laurentian University.

Aniuk, J. (2008). Review of The Dominion of Youth. *Journal of the History of Childhood and Youth, 1,* 301–303.

Anyon, J. (1980). Social class and the hidden curriculum of work. *Journal of Education, 162,* 67–92.

Apple, M. & Buras, K. (Eds). (2006). The subaltern speak: Curriculum, power and educational struggles. London: Routledge.

Arendt, H. (1958). *The Human Condition.* Chicago: University of Chicago Press.

Ariès, P. (1962). *Centuries of Childhood: A Social History of Family Life.* New York: Vintage Books.

Aristotle. (1987) *Rhetoric.* In G. Apostle (Ed.) *Aristotle Selected Works: Hippocrates.* Iowa: Peripatetic Press.

Arnett. J. (2010). Adolescence and emerging adulthood. New Jersey: Prentice Hall

Arnett, J.J. & Balle-Johnson, L. (1993) 'Cultural bases of risk behavior: Danish adolescents', *Child Development, 64,* 1842–55.

Arum, R. (2000). Schools and communities: Ecological and institutional dimensions. *Annual Review of Sociology, 26,* 395–418.

Assembly of First Nations. (2003). First Nations Regional Longitudinal Health Survey: Results for adults, youth and children living in First Nations. Ottawa: Assembly of First Nations.

Baudrillard, J. (1981). *For a Critique of the Political Economy of the Sign.* St. Louis: Telos.

———. (1993). *The Transparency of Evil.* Trans. James Benedict. London: Verso.

———. (1995). *The Gulf War Did Not Take Place.* Trans. Paul Patton. Bloomington: Indiana University Press.

———. (1996). *The Perfect Crime.* Trans. Chris Turner. London: Verso.

———. (2002a). *Screened Out.* Trans. Chris Turner. London: Verso.

———. (2002b). *The Spirit of Terrorism and Other Essays.* Trans. Chris Turner. London: Verso.

Beck, U. (1992). *Risk Society: Towards a New Modernity.* London: Sage.

Beder, S. (2009). *This Little Kiddy Went to Market: The Corporate Capture of Childhood.* New York: Pluto Press.

Bensen, P., Scales, P., Hamilton, S., & Sesma, A. (2006). Positive youth development: Theory, research and applications In W. Damon & R. Lerner (Eds), *Handbook of Child Psychology, 6th Edition.* New Jersey: John Wiley and Sons.

Berliner, David C. (2009). Poverty and Potential: Out-of-School Factors and School Success.

Bibby, R.W. (2001). *Canada's Teens: Today, Yesterday and Tomorrow.* Toronto: Stoddart Publishing.

Bibby, R.W. & Posterski, D.C. (1996). *Teen Trends: A Nation in Motion.* Toronto: Stoddard Publishing.

Blackstock, C. (2009). The occasional evil of angels: Learning from the experiences of Aboriginal peoples and social work. *First Peoples Child and Family Review, 4,* 28–37.

Blackstock, C., Clarke, J., Cullen, J., D'Hondt, J., & Formsa, J. (2004). Keeping the promise: The Convention on the Rights of the Child and the lived experiences of First Nations children and youth. Ottawa: First Nations Child & Family Caring Society.

Blanco, H., LeBrasseur, R., Lewko, J., Tilleczek, K., Volpe, R., Wilson, B-J., Duncan, A., & Keating, M. (2005). *Managing the health and safety interests of young workers in small businesses.* Report to the Workplace Safety and Insurance Board (wsib) Research Advisory Council.

Boulder and Tempe: *Education and the Public Interest Center & Education Policy Research Unit.* Retrieved [May 2010] from http://epicpolicy.org/publication/poverty-and-potential

Bowes, C. (2004). Culture Jamming: Confronting the Capitalist Colonization of Social Space. Master's Thesis, Laurentian University: Sudbury, ON.

Boyden, J. (2001). Childhood and the policy makers: A comparative perspective on the globalization of childhood. In A. Prout & A. James (Eds), *Constructing and Reconstructing Childhood* (pp. 190–229). London: RoutledgeFalmer.

Brake, M. (1985). *Comparative Youth Culture: The Sociology of Youth Cultures and Youth Subcultures in America, Britain, and Canada.* London: Routledge.

Bronfenbrenner, U. (1979). *The Ecology of Human Development.* Cambridge, MA: Harvard University Press.

———. (Ed.) (2005). *Making Human Beings Human: Bioecological Perspectives on Human Development.* Thousand Oaks California: Sage Publications.

Bruner, J. (1986). *Actual Minds, Possible Worlds.* Cambridge: Harvard University Press.

———. (1996). *The Culture of Education.* Cambridge: Harvard University Press.

———. (2004). Life as narrative. *Journal of Social Research, 71,* 691–710.

Camus, Albert. (1991). *The Rebel.* Trans. Anthony Bower. New York: Vintage Books.

———. (2007). *Christian Metaphysics and Neoplatonism.* Trans. With Introduction by Ronald D. Srigley. Columbia: University of Missouri Press.

Canadian Council on Learning (2007). *Redefining how success is measured in First Nations, Inuit and Metis learning.* Ottawa: Canadian Council on Learning.

Canadian Council on Learning (2009). The Video Game Debate: Bad for Behaviour, Good for Learning? Retrieved December 2009 from www.ccl-cca.ca/ccl

Canadian Council on Social Development (CCSD). (2006).The progress of Canada's children and youth. Retrieved May 2010 from www.ccsd.ca/pccy/2006/

Canadian Institute of Child Health (CICH). (2000). The Health of the Nova Scotia Mi'kmaq Population (1997), *The Health of Canada's Children: A CICH Profile* (3rd Ed.). Ottawa, ON: Canadian Institute of Child Health, p. 164.

Carr, R., Wright, J., & Brody, C. (1996). Effects of high school work experience a decade later: Evidence from a national longitudinal survey. *Sociology of Education, 69,* 66–81.

Carroll, W. (2004). *Critical Strategies for Social Research.* Toronto: Canadian Scholars' Press.

———. (2006). Marx's method and the contributions of institutional ethnography. In C. Frampton et al (Eds). *Sociology for changing the world: Social movements/social research.* Halifax: Fernwood Publishing.

Case. R. (1991). The mind's staircase: Exploring the conceptual underpinnings of children's thought and knowledge. Hillsdale, NJ: Erlbaum Associates Inc.

Case, R., Griffin, S., & Kelly, W. (1999). Socioeconomic gradients in mathematical ability and their responsiveness to intervention during early childhood. In D. Keating & C. Hertzman (Eds), *Developmental Health and the Wealth of Nations: Social, Biological and Educational Dynamics* (pp. 125–50). New York: Guildford Press.

Catterall, J. (1998). Risk and resilience in student transitions to high school. *American Journal of Education, 106,* 302–333.

Chandler, M. & Lalonde, C. (2008) Cultural continuity as a protective factor against suicide in First Nations youth. *Horizons: Special Issue on Aboriginal Youth, Hope or Heartbreak: Aboriginal Youth and Canada's Future. 10,* 68–72.

———. (1998). Cultural continuity as a hedge against suicide in Canada's First Nations. *Transcultural Psychiatry, 35,* 191–219.

Cheng. (1995). Issues related to student part-time work: What did the research find in the Toronto situation and other contexts? Research Report of the Toronto Board of Education. Toronto: Toronto Board of Education Research Services.

Chisholm, L. (2006). European youth research: Development, debates and demands. *New Directions for Child and Adolescent Development, 113,* 11–21.

Cohen, P. (1999). *Rethinking the Youth Question: Education, Labour and Cultural Studies.* Durham: Duke University Press.

Cohen, P. & Ainley, P. (2000). In the country of the blind: Youth studies and cultural studies in Britain. In J. Pickford (Ed.). *Youth Justice: Theory and Practice.* London: Cavendish Publishing Ltd.

Cohn, N. (1995). *Cosmos, Chaos, and the World to Come: The Ancient Roots of Apocalyptic Faith.* New Haven: Yale University Press.

Comacchio, C. (2006). *The Dominion of Youth: Adolescence and the Making of a Modern Canada, 1920 to 1950.* Waterloo, ON: Wilfrid Laurier University Press.

Cooper, B. (1991). *Action into Nature: An Essay on the Meaning of Technology.* Notre Dame: University of Notre Dame Press.

Côté, J. (1992). Was Mead wrong about coming of age in Samoa? An analysis of the Mead/Freeman controversy for scholars of adolescence and human development. *Journal of Youth and Adolescence, 21,* 1–29.

———. (1994). Adolescent storm and stress: An evaluation of the Mead/Freeman controversy. Hillsdale: Lawrence Erlbaum.

———. (2000). *Arrested Adulthood: The Changing Nature of Maturity and Identity.* New York: New York University Press.

Côté, J. & Allahar, A. (2006). *Critical Youth Studies: A Canadian Focus.* Toronto: Pearson Ltd.

Csikszentmihalyi, M. & Schneider, B. (2000). *Becoming Adult: How Teenagers Prepare for the World of Work.* New York: Basic Books.

Culture jamming, retrieved January 2010 from www.stayfreemagazine.org/9/adbusters.htm.

Dale, S. (1996). McLuhan's children: The Greenpeace message and the media. Toronto: Between the Lines Press.

Damon, W. (2004).What is positive youth development? *Annals of the American Academy of Political and Social Science. 591,* 13–23.

Davies, S & Guppy, N. (2006). *The Schooled Society.* Toronto: Oxford University Press.

Demos, J. & Demos, V. (1969). Adolescence in historical perspective. *Journal of Marriage and the Family, 31,* 632–638.

Dewey, J. (1938). *Experience and Education.* New York: Touchstone Press.

Dyer-Witheford. (2003). *Digital Play: The Interaction of Technology, Culture, and Marketing* (with Greig de Peuter and Stephen Kline). Montreal: McGill-Queen's University Press..s

Elder, G.H., Jr. (1995). The life course paradigm: Social change and individual development. In P. Moen, G.H. Elder, Jr., & K. Lüscher, *Examining lives in context: Perspectives on the ecology of human development.* Washington: APA Press.

Enright, R.D., Levy, V., Harris, D., & Lapsley, D. (1987). Do economic conditions influence how theorists view adolescents? *Journal of Youth and Adolescence, 16,* 541–559.

Erikson, E.H. (1958). *Young Man Luther: A Study in Psychoanalysis and History.* New York: W.W. Norton.

Feixa, C., Pereira, I. & Juris, J. (2009). Global citizenship and the 'new, new' social movements: Iberian connections. *Young 17,* 421.

Feyerabend, P. (1995). *Killing time: An autobiography of Paul Feyerabend.* Chicago: University of Chicago Press.

———. (1999). *Conquest of abundance: A tale of abstraction versus the richness of being.* Chicago: University of Chicago Press.

Foucault, M. (1977). *Discipline and punish: The birth of the prison.* New York: Vintage.

Fogel, A., Lyra, M. & Valsier, J. (1997). Introduction: Perspectives on indeterminism and development. In J. Valsiner (Ed.) *Dynamics and indeterminism in developmental and social processes.* New Jersey: Lawrence Erlbaum Associates.

Frampton, C., Kinman, G., Thomson, A.K. & Tilleczek, K. (2006). *Sociology for changing the world: Social movements/Social research.* Halifax: Fernwood Press.

Frank, A. (1991). *The diary of a young girl: the definitive edition.* O. Frank and M. Pressler (Eds). New York: Bantam books.

Freire. (1970). *Pedagogy of the oppressed.* New York: Continuum.

Frone, M. (1998). Predictors of work injuries among employed adolescents. *Journal of Applied Psychology. 83,* 565–576.

Fukuyama, F. (2002) *Our Posthuman Future: Consequences of the Biotechnology Revolution.* New York: Picador.

Furlong, A. (2008). Refocusing on disengagement. In K. Tilleczek (Ed.) *Why do students drop out of high school? Narrative studies and social critiques.* New York: Edwin Mellen Press.

Furlong, A. & Cartmel, F. (2007). *Young People and Social Change: New Perspectives.* Berkshire: Open University Press.

Garbarino, J. (1990). The human ecology of risk. In S.J. Meisels & J.P. Shonkoff (Eds), *Handbook of early intervention.* (pp. 78–96). New York: Cambridge University Press.

Garmezy, N. (1991).Resilience in children's adaptation to negative life events and stressed environments. *Pediatric Annals, 20,* 461.

Giddens, A. (1976). *New rules of sociological method.* London: Hutchinson & Company.

Gillis, J.R. (1981). *Youth and history* (2nd ed.). New York: Academic Press.

Goffman. I. (1969). Strategic interaction. Pennsylvania: University of Pennsylvania Press.

Grant, G. (1969). *Technology and Empire.* Toronto: House of Anansi Press.

Griffen, C. (1993). *Representations of Youth: The Study of Youth and Adolescence in Britain and America.* Oxford: Polity Press.

———. (1997). Representations of the young, in *Youth and Society,* J. Roche & S. Tucker (Eds), London: Sage Publications.

Griffith, A. (1995). Mothering, school, and children's development. In M. Campbell & A. Mancion (Eds.), *Knowledge, Experience and Ruling Relations.* Toronto: University of Toronto Press.

Gullone, E., Moore, S., Moss, S. & Boyd, C. (2000). The adolescent risk-taking questionnaire: development and psychometric evaluation, *Journal of Adolescent Research, 15* (2), 231–50.

Hall, G. (1904). *Adolescence.* New York: Appleton.

Health Canada. (2006). Young people in Canada: Their health and well-being, Ottawa: Health Canada.

———. (1997). For the Safety of Canadian Children and Youth: From Injury Data to Preventative Measures. Minister of Public Works, Ottawa.

Hendrick, H. (2001). Constructions and reconstructions of British childhood: An interpretive survey, 1800 to the present. In A. Prout & A. James (Eds), *Constructing and Reconstructing Childhood* (pp. 34–62). London: RoutledgeFalmer.

Ipos Reid Poll (2004). Canadian inter@ctive Reid Report. Retrieved May 2010 at www.ipsos.ca/reid/interactive/index.cfm

Irwin, C. (1993) Adolescents and risk taking: how are they related?, in N. Bell & R. Bell (Eds), *Adolescent Risk Taking* (pp. 7–28). Newbury Park, CA: Sage Publications.

Ito, M., Horst, H., Bittani., B., Boyd, D., et al. (2008). *Living and learning with new media: Summary and findings from the Digital Youth Project.* Chicago: MacArthur Foundation.

James, A. & Prout, A. (2001). *Constructing*

and Reconstructing Childhood London: RoutledgeFalmer.

Jelalian, E., Spirito, A. & Rasile, D. (1997). Risk taking, reported injury and perception of future injury among adolescents, *Journal of Pediatric Psychology 22*, 513–31.

Jenks, C. (1996a). *Childhood*. New York: Routledge.

Kaiser Family Foundation. (2010). *Generation M²: Media in the Lives of 8 to 18 year olds.* California: Henry J. Kaiser Family Foundation.

Keating, D. (1996). Habits of mind for a learning society: Educating for human development. In D. Olson and N. Torrence (Eds), *Handbook of education and human development: New models of learning, teaching, and schooling.* Oxford: Blackwell.

Keating, D. (1998). Looking for trouble: new slant on adolescent risk-taking, *Journal of Applied Developmental Psychology*, 19, 663–67.

Keating, D. (1999). The learning society: A human development agenda. In D. Keating & C. Hertzman (Eds), *Developmental Health and the Wealth of Nations: Social, Biological and Educational Dynamics* (pp. 237–51). New York: Guildford Press.

Keating, D. & Hertzman, C. (1999). Modernity's paradox. In D. Keating & C. Hertzman (Eds.), *Developmental Health and the Wealth of Nations: Social, Biological and Educational Dynamics* (pp. 1–17). New York: Guildford Press.

Keating, D. & Mustard, F. (1993). Social economic factors and human development. In D. Ross (Ed.). *Family security in insecure times*. Ottawa: National Forum on Family Security.

Kelly, P. (2000). The dangerousness of youth-at-risk: The possibilities of surveillance and intervention in uncertain times. *Journal of Adolescence, 23*, 463–476.

Kett, J.F. (1977). *Rites of Passage: Adolescence in America 1790 to the Present*. New York: Basic Books.

Kiecolt-Glaser, J. et al. (1995). Slowing the wound healing of psychological stress. *The Lancet, 346*, 1194–1196.

Kinsman, G. (2006). Mapping social relations of struggle: Activism, ethnography and social organization. In C. Frampton et al. (Eds). *Sociology for changing the world: Social movements/social research*. Halifax: Fernwood Publishing.

Klein, N. (2000). *No Logo: Taking Aim at the Brand Bullies*. Toronto: Knopf Canada.

Krahn, H. (1991). Youth employment. In R. Barnhorst and L. Johnson (Eds), *The state of the child in Ontario*. Toronto: Oxford University Press.

Kusum, S. (1998). Part-time employment in high school and its effect on academic achievement. *Journal of Educational Research, 91*, 131–9.

Larson, R (2000). Toward a psychology of positive youth development. American Psychologist, 55, 170–83.

Lasn, K. (1999). *Culture Jam: How to Reverse America's Suicidal Consumer Binge—And Why We Must*. New York: HarperCollins.

Latham, R. (2002). *Consuming Youth: Vampires, Cyborgs and the Culture of Consumption*. Chicago: University of Chicago Press.

Lawler, S. (2002). Narrative in social research. In T. May (Ed.), *Qualitative research in action*. California: Sage Publications.

Layne, L., et al. (1994). Adolescent occupational injuries requiring hospital emergency department treatment: A national representative sample. *American Journal of Public Health, 4*, 657–660.

Lee, N. (1998). *Towards and immature sociology*. Oxford: Blackwell Publishers.

Leidner, R. (2003). *Fast food, fast talk: Service work and the routinization of everyday life*. California: University of California Press.

Lerner, R.M. (Ed.). (2002). *Concepts and theories of human development*. Mahwah, NJ: Erlbaum.

Levine, E. (1993*). Freedom's children: Young civil rights activists tell their own stories*. New York: Avon Books.

Levitt, M. & Selman, R. (1996). The personal meaning of risk behaviour. A developmental perspective on friendship and fighting in early adolescence. In. G. Noam and K. Fisher (Eds.) *Development and vulnerability in close personal relationships*. Mahwah, NJ: Lawrence Erlbaum Associates, Inc.

Levitt, M.Z., Selman, R. & Richmond, L.J. (1991). The psychosocial foundations of early adolescent's high-risk behaviour: Implications for theory and practice. *Journal of Research on Adolescence, 1(4)*, 349–78.

Lightfoot, C. (1997). *The Culture of Adolescent Risk Taking*. New York: Guilford Press.

Lightfoot, C. & Cox, B. (1997). Locating competence: the sociogenesis of mind and the problem of internalization, in B. Cox & C. Lightfoot (Eds) *Sociogenetic Perspectives on Internalization*. Mahwah, NJ: Lawrence Erlbaum.

Lincoln, Y. & Guba, E. (2000). Paradigmatic controversies, contradictions and emerging confluences. In N. Denzin & Y. Lincoln (Eds), *Handbook of qualitative research*. California: Sage Publications.

Loughlin, C. & Barling, J. (1999). The nature of youth employment. In J. Barling and K. Kelloway (Eds), *Young workers: Varieties of experience*. Washington, DC: The American Psychological Association.

Luthar, S (2006). Resilience in development: A synthesis of research across five decades. In

D. Cicchetti & D. Cohen, (Eds), *Developmental psychopathology: Risk, disorder and adaptation*. New York: Wiley.

Lyng, S. (1993). Dysfunctional risk-taking: criminal behaviour as edgework. In N. Bell & R. Bell (Eds), *Adolescent Risk Taking*. London: Sage.

Manning, W. (1990). Parenting employed teenagers. *Youth and Society, 22*,184–200.

Marecek, J. (2002). *Safe conduct: dangers, pleasures and adolescent sexuality*, 32nd Annual Meeting of the Jean Piaget Society. Philadelphia, PA, 6–8 June.

Marsh, H. (1991). Employed during high school: Character building or a subversion of academic goals? *Sociology of Education, 64*, 172–189.

Mayhew, D.R. & Simpson, H.M. (2002). The safety value of driver education and training, *Injury Prevention, 8*, 13–118, McLuhan, M. (1994). *Understanding Media: The Extensions of Man*. Cambridge: MIT Press.

McNally, D. (2002). Another world is possible: Globalizatoin and anti-capitalism. Winnipeg: Arrbeiter Ring Publications.

Mead, M. (1928). *Coming of Age in Samoa*. New York: W. Morrow and Company.

Media Awareness Network. (2001). Young Canadians in a wired world. Phase I. Retrieved May 2010 from www.media-awareness.ca/english/research/YCWW/Phase I.

Media Awareness Network. (2005). Young Canadians in a wired world: Phase II. Retrieved May 2010 from www.media-awareness.ca/english/research/YCWW/Phase II.

Mitterauer, M. (1993). *A History of Youth*. Oxford: Blackwell.

Modell, J. & Goodman, M. (1990). Historical perspectives. In S.S. Feldman & G.R. Elliott (Eds), *At the Threshold: The Developing Adolescent* (pp. 93–122). Cambridge: Harvard University Press.

Moore, E. & Parsons, J. (2000) A research agenda for adolescent risk-taking: where do we go from here?, *Journal of Adolescence, 23*, 371–6.

Mortimer, J., Finsh, M., Ryu, S. & Shanahan. M. (1991). *Evidence from a prospective longitudinal study of work experience, adolescent mental health and behavioural adjustment*. Paper presented at the Biennial Meeting of the Society for Research in Child Development, Seattle, Washington.

Moskowitz, S. (2004). American youth in the workplace. Legal aberration, failed social policy. *Albany Law Review, 67*, 1071–1096.

Mueller, M., Tilleczek, K., Rummens, J.A., & Boydell, K. (2008). Methodological considerations for the study of youth and school disengagement. In K. Tilleczek (Ed.), *Why Do Students Drop Out of High School? Narrative Studies and Social Critiques*. New York: Edwin Mellen Press.

Murdoch, I. (1070). *The sovereignty of the good*. London: Routledge.

Muus, R.E. & Porton, H.D. (1998). *Adolescent Behaviour in Society: A Book of Readings*. New York: McGraw-Hill.

Newman, K. (1999). *No shame in my game: The working poop in the inner city*. New York: Knopf.

Nussbaum, M. (2010). *Not for profit: Why democracy needs the humanities*. New Jersey: Princeton University Press. Oatley. (2003).

Ontario Ministry of Transportation (MTO). (2000). Ontario Road Safety Annual Report, Toronto: MTO.

Ontario Tobacco Research Unit. (1997). *Special report on youth and tobacco in Ontario 1997: A cause for concern*. Toronto: Ontario Tobacco Research Unit.

Pais, J. (2003). The multiple faces of the future in the labyrinth of life. *Journal of Youth Studies, 6*, 115–26.

Pertraitis, J., Flay, B., & Miller, T. (1995). Reviewing theories of adolescent substance use: Organizing pieces of the puzzle. *Psychological Bulletin, 117*, 67–86.

Piaget, J. (1958). The adolescent as a total personality. In B. Inhelder & J. Piaget, *The Growth of Logical Thinking*. New York: Basic Books.

———. (1972). Intellectual evolution from adolescence to adulthood, *Human Development, 15*, 1–12.

Putnam, R. (2000). *Bowling alone: The collapse and revival of the American community*. New York: Simon and Shuster.

Qvortrup, J. (2001). A voice for children in statistical and social accounting: A plea for children's rights to be heard. In A. Prout & A. James (Eds), *Constructing and Reconstructing Childhood* (pp. 85–106). London: RoutledgeFalmer.

Rojeck, C. (1985). *Capitalism and leisure theory*. London: Tavistock.

Ross, C. & Wu, C. (1995). The links between education and health. *American Sociological Review, 60*, 719–45.

Rothe, J.P. (2000). *Undertaking qualitative research: Concepts and cases in injury, health and social life*. Edmonton: University of Alberta Press.

Rutter, M. (1994). Continuities, transitions and turning points in development. In M. Rutter & D. Hay (Eds.) *Development through life: A handbook for clinicians*. London: Blackwell Scientific.

Santor, D., Short, K., & Ferguson, B. (2009). Taking mental health to school: A policy-oriented paper on school-based mental health for Ontario. Ottawa: Provincial Centre for Excellence in Child and Youth Mental Health.

Schissel, B. (1997). *Blaming Children: Youth Crime, Moral Panics and the Politics of Hate*. Halifax: Fernwood Publishing.

————. (2007). *Still Blaming Children: Youth Crime, Moral Panics and the Politics of Hate*. Halifax: Fernwood Publishing.

Schonert-Reichl, K. (2000). *Children and youth at risk: Some conceptual considerations*. Paper presented at pan-Canadian Education Research Symposium on children and youth at risk. Ottawa: HRSDC.

Schor, J. (2004). *Born to buy: The commercialized child and the new consumer culture*. New York: Scribner.

Schorr, L. (1989). *Within our reach: Breaking the cycle of disadvantage*. New York: Doubleday.

Schwandt, T. (2007). *Dictionary of Qualitative Inquiry* (3rd Ed.). Los Angeles: Sage Publications.

Sebald, H. (1992). *Adolescence: A social psychological analysis*. New York: Prentice-Hall.

Smink, J., Schargel, F.P. (2004). Helping Students Graduate: A Strategic Approach to Dropout Prevention. Larchmont, NY: Eye on Education.

Smith, D. (2002). Institutional ethnography, in T. May (Ed.), *Qualitative Research in Action*, London: Sage Publications.

Smith, G. (1998). The ideology of 'fag': The school experience of gay students. *The Sociological Quarterly, 2*, 309–35.

Smith, L. (2004). *Decolonizing methodologies: Research and indigenous peoples*. London: Zed Books.

Smyth & Hattam. (2001). 'Voiced' research as a sociology for understanding dropping out of school, *British Journal of the Sociology of Education, 22*, 401–15.

Srigley, R. (forthcoming, 2011). *Greece in Rags: Albert Camus' Critique of Modernity*. Columbia: University of Missouri Press.

Srigley, R. & Tilleczek, K. (2008). *Modernity's Youth: Images of Rebellion from the Cave*. Paper presented at the International Sociological Association Forum on Sociology, Growing Up in a Liquid World: The Debating of Youth Questions. Barcelona, Spain, Sept 6.

Statistics Canada. (1998). *Health reports*. Ottawa: Statistics Canada Catalogue #82–003-XPB.

Statistics Canada. (2003). Canadian Labour Force Survey.

Steinberg, L., Fegley, S., & Dornbusch, S. (1993). Negative impact of part-time work on adolescent adjustment: Evidence from a longitudinal study. *Developmental Psychology, 29*, 171–180.

Stephens, T. & Stephens, C. (1996). *Readiness to quit smoking among Canadian smokers*. Ottawa: National Clearinghouse on Tobacco and Health.

Suomi, S. (1999). Developmental trajectories, early experiences, and community consequences: Lessons from studies with rhesus monkeys. In D. Keating & C. Hertzman (Eds), *Developmental Health and the Wealth of Nations: Social, Biological and Educational Dynamics* (pp. 185–200). New York: Guildford Press.

Sutherland, N. Barmon, J. & Hale, L. (1992). History of children and youth: A bibliography. Connecticut: Greenwood Publishing Group.

Swidler, A. (1986). Culture in action: Symbols and strategies. *American Sociological Review, 51*, 273–86.

Tannock, S. (2001). *Youth at work: The unionized and fast food grocery work place*. Philadelphia: Temple University Press.

Tapscott. D. (2009). *Grown up digital: How the net generation is changing your world*. New York: McGraw Hill.

Tilleczek, K. (2004). The illogic of youth driving culture. *The Journal of Youth Studies, 7* (4), 473–99.

————. (2007a). *Having a terrible time, wish you were here: Post cards from high school*. Paper presentation at the Atlantic Educators Conference, University of Prince Edward Island, Charlottetown, Canada. October 24–26.

————. (2007b). *Fresh Starts/False Starts: A Review of Literature on the Transition from Elementary to Secondary School*. Invited policy paper prepared for the Ontario Ministry of Education, Toronto, Ontario.

————. (2008a). Building bridges for young people: Transitions from elementary to secondary school. *Education Canada, 68*–71.

————. (2008b). The failing health of children and youth in Northern Ontario. In D. Leadbeater (Ed.), *Mining Town Crises: Globalization, Labour and Resistance in Sudbury, Canada*. Halifax: Fernwood Press.

————. (2008c). *Poverty and Early School Leaving: Addressing 'What Works'?* Invited policy paper prepared for the Ontario Ministry of Child and Youth Services, Toronto, Ontario.

————. (Ed.). (2008d). *Why Do Students Drop Out of High School? Narrative Studies and Social Critiques*. New York: Edwin Mellen Press.

————. (2008e). *Restoring the balance of education: Aboriginal youth, human rights and health*. Invited Education Expert Panellist at Conference of Aboriginal Education and Human Rights: The Case of Attawapiskat. Toronto: University of Toronto, November 26, 2008.

————. (2009). *Being and Becoming in Bodies: A Discussion of Adolescent Puberty and Risk Behaviour*. Invited discussant at the Successful Transitions Conference. Human Resource and Social Development Canada. Ottawa, April 28–29.

———. (in press). Adjusting the rear view mirror: An examination of youth driving culture. In *Youth and Society*. Sage Publications.

Tilleczek, K. & Ferguson, B. (2007). *Transitions from Elementary to Secondary School: A Review and Synthesis of the Literature*. Toronto: Hospital for Sick Children (Report the Ontario Ministry of Education).

Tilleczek, K., Ferguson, B., Roth Edney, D., Rummens, J. A., Boydell, K. & Mueller, M.P. (2008). Reconstructing school leaving: A sociological view from the margins. In Tilleczek, K. (Ed.), *Why Do Students Drop Out of High School? Narrative Studies and Social Critiques*. New York: Edwin Mellen Press.

Tilleczek, K. & Hine, D. W. (2006). The personal meaning of smoking as health and social risk in adolescence. *Journal of Adolescence, 29* (2), 273–87.

Tilleczek K., Laflamme, S., Ferguson, B., Roth Edney, D., Cudney, D., Girard, M. & Cardoso, S. (2008). *Hope and Fear in the Elementary Years: A Report of Phase I of Mapping the Processes and Pathways of Transitions from Elementary to Secondary School*. Toronto: Hospital for Sick Children (Report to the Ontario Ministry of Education).

———. (2009). *Crossing the River to Secondary School: A Report of Phase II of Mapping the Processes and Pathways of Transitions from Elementary to Secondary School*. Toronto: Hospital for Sick Children (Report to the Ontario Ministry of Education).

———. (2010). *Fresh Starts and False Starts: Young People in Transitions from Elementary to Secondary School*. Toronto: Hospital for Sick Children (Report to the Ontario Ministry of Education).

Tilleczek, K. & Lewko, J.H. (2001). Factors influencing the pursuit of health and science career pathways for Canadian adolescents in transition from school to work. *Journal of Youth Studies, 4* (4), 415–28.

Tjepkema, M. (2002). The health of the off-reserve Aboriginal populations. Supplement to Health Repots, Catalogue 82-003-SIE. Ottawa: Statistics Canada.

Transport Canada. (2001). *Canadian motor vehicle traffic collision statistics*. Available from www.tc.gc.ca/raodsafety. Retrieved June 2010 at www.tc.gc.ca/eng/roadsafety/tp-tp 3322-2003-menu-630.htm

Trembley, P. (2010). Youth Suicide Problems, Gay/Bisexual Male Focus, Retrieved May 2010 from www.youth-suicide.com/gay-bisexual/.

Tyyska, V. (2009). *Youth and Society: The Long and Winding Road*. Toronto: Canadian Scholars Press.

Unger, M. (2004). *Nurturing hidden resilience in troubled youth*. Toronto: University of Toronto Press.

———. (2008). A brief overview of resilience: How does the concept help us to understand children's positive development under stress? Paper presented to the Learning Partnership for the National Dialogue on Resilience in Youth. Winnipeg, November 2008.

Voegelin, Eric. (1990). *The Collected Works of Eric Voegelin*, Volume 12, *Published Essays, 1966–1985*. Baton Rouge: Louisiana State University Press.

Vygotsky, L.S. (1929). *The problem of the cultural development of the child*. Retrieved August, 2004, from www.marxists.org/archive/vygotsky/.

———. (1978). *Mind in Society: The Development of Higher Psychological Processes*. Trans. M. Cole, V. John-Steiner, S. Scribner, E. Souberman. Cambridge, MA: Harvard University Press.

———. (1986). *Thought and Language*. Cambridge, MA: MIT Press.

Ward, K., Klesges, R. & Halpern, M. (1997). Predictors of smoking cessation and sate of the art smoking interventions. *Journal of Social Issues, 53*, 129–45.

Werner, E. & Smith, R. (1992). Overcoming the odds: High-risk children from birth to adulthood. Ithaca, NY: Cornell University Press.

Willms, D. (1999). Quality and inequality in children's literacy: The effects of family, schools and communities. In D. Keating & C. Hertzman (Eds), *Developmental Health and the Wealth of Nations: Social, Biological and Educational Dynamics* (pp. 72–93). New York: Guildford Press.

———. (Ed.). (2002). *Vulnerable children: Findings from the National Longitudinal Study of Children and Youth*. Edmonton: University of Alberta Press.

———. (2003). *Student engagement at school: A sense of belonging and participation*. PISA: Organization for Economic Co-operation and Development.

———. (2009). *Synthesis and policy implications: Successful transitions conference*. Paper presented at Successful Transitions Conference, Human Resources and Skills Development Canada, Ottawa, April 28–29, 2009.

Willms, D., Friesen, S. & Milton, P. (2009). What did you do in school today? Transforming classrooms through social, academic and intellectual achievement. (First National Report). Toronto: Canadian Education Association.

World Health Organization. (1946). Preamble to the Constitution of the World Health

Organization as adopted at the International Health Conference, New York, June 19–22. (Official Records of the World Health Organization, No. 2:100).

———. (1999). *Injury: A leading cause of the global burden of disease.* Geneva, Switzerland: World Health Organization.

———. (2003). *Strategic directions for improving the health and development of children and adolescents.* Geneva: World Health Organization.

World Health Organization and Health Canada. (2004). Trends in the health of Canadian youth—Young People in Canada, Their health and well-being. Ottawa: Health Canada.

Wyn, J., & White, R. (2008). *Youth and Society: Exploring the Social Dynamics of Youth Experience.* Melbourne: Oxford University Press.

Youniss, J., Yates, M. & Su, Y. (1997). Social integration: community service and marijuana use in high school seniors, *Journal of Adolescent Research, 12* (2), 245–62.

Youniss, J., McLellan, J. & Mazer, B. (2001). Voluntary service, peer group orientation and civic engagement, *Journal of Adolescent Research.* 16, 456–68.

Youniss, J., Bales, S., et al. (2002). Youth civic engagement in the twenty-first century. *Journal of Research in Adolescence, 12,* 121–48.

Youniss, J. (2006). G. Stanley Hall and his times: Too much so, yet not enough. History of Psychology, 9, 224–35.

Glossary

Agency The ability of individuals to make independent choices and act on their own behalf and on behalf of others. Agency is a social process of resistance and a manner of acting in a collective sense to either reinforce or resist culture.

Axiology The study of quality or value, in this case, of research; ethics.

Becoming One of the fundamental social processes of youth development. It relates to the nonlinear and complex processes of similarity and change over time: physical, emotional, social, cultural, and intellectual.

Being One of the fundamental social processes of youth development. It relates to living in the moment of time and experience and to identify processes.

Belonging One of the fundamental social processes of youth development. It relates to the importance of being accepted and included and making friends. Issues of status and social comparison are important aspects of inclusion for youth. Belonging is related to being a part of something (school, family, community, friends, peer groups, etc.); social exclusion is the flip side of this.

Chronosystem In Bronfenbrenner's bioecological approach, the system that captures the way changes in environmental systems, such as social trends and life events, are patterned over a person's lifetime.

Commodification The process of attaching a monetary value to human activities. In this case, it refers to the ways in which the search for 'youth' itself is for sale via plastic surgery and so forth. In addition, the energy and vitality of young people is co-opted by the market and their time is spent 'buying' as opposed to other youthful activities.

Complex cultural nesting approach The framework posited in this book whereby many levels of social influence surround the young person and whereby institutions are nested within each of these systems (history, culture, community, family, school, etc.). The development of youth takes place in these nested social contexts and the fundamental social processes of being, becoming, and belonging are integral to them.

Critical discourse analysis (CDA) An approach in youth studies that involves the critical reading of texts that make up our social locations. It is concerned with studying and analyzing written texts and spoken words to understand their particular meaning within a specific context.

Critical ethnography A method that focuses on the perspectives of marginalized people in society, providing them an opportunity to tell their own stories and examining those stories for underlying influences of domination or power.

Cultural nests Places of belonging or marginalization, such as family, home, school, community, etc. Nests exist within other nests and the idea that transitions are "nested" is an important one since young people move along their pathways from childhood to adulthood while at the same time they move between schools, make social, emotional and physical developments, and so forth.

Culture The shared beliefs, values, meanings, languages, and norms of groups of people. These are generally thought to be passed on over generations and can be both material and non-material. In each case, these aspects of culture can be seen in the daily lives of young people are they are enacted in their every day actions in schools, communities, work places, with friends etc.

Epistemology The theory of knowledge, or how we come to know what we know.

Institutional ethnography (IE) A sociological method of inquiry that explores the social relations that structure people's everyday lives. For the institutional ethnographer, ordinary daily activity becomes the site for an investigation of social organization. It is a method for mapping the translocal relations that coordinate people's activities within institutions.

Liminality The cognitive and emotional state and experience of being in-between; neither here nor there.

Macrosystem In Bronfenbrenner's bioecological approach, the larger cultural or subcultural context of development. Patterns, consistencies, and inconsistencies in the form and content of micro and meso systems, for example, globalization, poverty, educational policy.

Marginalization The social process of being made marginal; to be relegated to the outer edges of a society or culture.

Mesosystem In Bronfenbrenner's bioecological approach, interrelationships between microsystems or immediate environments (for example, ways in which events in the family affect a child's interactions at a daycare centre). The interrelations between people in two or more settings in which the young person actively participates, for example, the relations among home, school, neighbourhood, peer group.

Microsystem In Bronfenbrenner's bioecological approach, the immediate settings in which the person functions (for example, the family). A pattern of activities, roles, and interpersonal relations experienced by young people in a given setting with particular physical and material characteristics, for example, homes, the family, the classroom, etc.

Nested transitions The concept that transitions do not happen in isolation and that young people can be undergoing several transitions at any given time. For example, young people may move from elementary to secondary school while at the same time transitioning from childhood to adulthood as well as transitioning through their communities and families and into the labour market.

Ontology The branch of metaphysics that deals with how we understand the nature of reality, of being; in social research methods, a theory of how the social world comes into being.

Participatory action research (PAR) Research that focuses on co-operation and collaboration between the researchers and other participants in all aspects of the research process. PAR is based on democratic ideals or principles and has a dual objective of producing knowledge and action.

Praxis The meeting of theory and method-ology and practice—putting theory into action.

Resilience In Luthar's work, defined as 'a phenomenon or process reflecting relatively positive adaptation despite experiences of significant adversity or trauma'; the ability to recover from trauma or stress. In Chapter 1, resilient youth are defined as those who remain competent despite predicted patterns of misfortune and stress.

Storm and stress G. S. Hall's term for the emotional ups and downs and rapid changes that he believed characterize adolescence.

Subaltern studies An approach that is focused more on what happens among the masses at the base levels of society than among the elite.

Theory A set of concepts and propositions designed to organize, describe, and explain a set of observations. Theories are attempted as coherent and elegant stories about some set of ideas and observations.

Credits

Grateful acknowledgement is made for permission to reprint the following:

Page 3: Griffen, C. (1997). Representations of the young, in Youth and Society, eds J. Roche & S. Tucker, London: Sage Publications. Griffen, C. (1997). Representations of the young, in Youth and Society, eds J. Roche & S. Tucker, London: Sage Publications.

Page 3: Cohen & Ainley. (2000). In the country of the blind: Youth studies and cultural studies in Britain. In J. Pickford (Ed.). *Youth Justice: Theory and Practice*. London: Cavendish Publishing Ltd.

Page 7: The First Nations Lifelong Learning Model has been developed by the Canadian Council on Learning (CCL) with the University of Saskatchewan's Aboriginal Education Research Centre and the First Nations Adult Higher Education Consortium (co-leads of CCL's Aboriginal Learning Knowledge Centre) in partnership with Aboriginal learning experts and the National Aboriginal Organizations in Canada, as identified at www.ccl-cca.ca/CCL/Reports/RedefiningSuccessInAboriginalLearning/RedefiningSuccessPartners.htm, and is reproduced with permission.

Page 20: Furlong, A. & Cartmel, F. (2007). *Young People and Social Change: New Perspectives*. Berkshire: Open University Press. Reproduced with the kind permission of Open University Press. All rights reserved.

Pages 21–2: Furlong, A. & Cartmel, F. (2007). *Young People and Social Change: New Perspectives*. Berkshire: Open University Press.

Page 23: Margaret Mead, *Coming of Age in Samoa*.

Page 43: Furlong, A. & Cartmel, F. (2007). *Young People and Social Change: New Perspectives*. Berkshire: Open University Press.

Pages 43–4: Furlong, A. & Cartmel, F. (2007). *Young People and Social Change: New Perspectives*. Berkshire: Open University Press.

Page 44: Furlong, A. & Cartmel, F. (2007). *Young People and Social Change: New Perspectives*. Berkshire: Open University Press.

Page 45: Griffen, C. (1997). Representations of the young, in Youth and Society, eds J. Roche & S. Tucker, London: Sage Publications. Griffen, C. (1997). Representations of the young, in Youth and Society, eds J. Roche & S. Tucker, London: Sage Publications.

Page 46: Cohen & Ainley. (2000). In the country of the blind: Youth studies and cultural studies in Britain. In J. Pickford (Ed.). *Youth Justice: Theory and Practice*. London: Cavendish Publishing Ltd.

Page 56: Blackstock 2009.

Page 57: Source: First Nations Regional Longitudinal Health Survey (RHS) 2002–03. Results for Adults, Youth and Children Living in First Nations Communities. The First Nations Information Governance Centre, November 2005.

Page 66: Latham, R. (2002a). The cybernetic vampire of consumer youth culture. In *Consuming Youth: Vampires, Cyborgs and the Culture of Consumption* (pp. 1–25). Chicago: University of Chicago Press.

Page 66: Furlong, A. & Cartmel, F. (2007). *Young People and Social Change: New Perspectives*. Berkshire: Open University Press.

Page 79: Latham, R. (2002a). The cybernetic vampire of consumer youth culture. In *Consuming Youth: Vampires, Cyborgs and the Culture of Consumption* (pp. 1–25). Chicago: University of Chicago Press.

Page 80: Furlong, A. & Cartmel, F. (2007). *Young People and Social Change: New Perspectives*. Berkshire: Open University Press.

Pages 81–2: Furlong (2008).

Page 94: Furlong (2008).

Page 96: Furlong (2008).

Page 101: Tilleczek K., Laflamme, S., Ferguson, B., Roth Edney, D., Cudney, D., Girard, M. & Cardoso, S. (2009). *Crossing the River to Secondary School: A Report of Phase II of Mapping the Processes and Pathways of Transitions from Elementary to Secondary School*. Toronto: Hospital for Sick

Children (Report to the Ontario Ministry of Education).

Page 109: Tilleczek, K. & Ferguson, B. (2007). *Transitions from Elementary to Secondary School: A Review and Synthesis of the Literature.* Toronto: Hospital for Sick Children (Report the Ontario Ministry of Education).

Page 111: Tilleczek K., Laflamme, S., Ferguson, B., Roth Edney, D., Cudney, D., Girard, M. & Cardoso, S. (2009). *Crossing the River to Secondary School: A Report of Phase II of Mapping the Processes and Pathways of Transitions from Elementary to Secondary School.* Toronto: Hospital for Sick Children (Report to the Ontario Ministry of Education).

Page 128: Griffen, C. (1997). Representations of the young, in Youth and Society, eds J. Roche & S. Tucker, London: Sage Publications. Griffen, C. (1997). Representations of the young, in Youth and Society, eds J. Roche & S. Tucker, London: Sage Publications.

Page 131: Community Health Systems Resource Group (CHSRG) of the Hospital for Sick Children

Pages 133–4: Feixa, C., Pereira, I., & Juris, J. (2009). Global citizenship and the 'new, new' social movements: Iberian connections. *Young 17*, 421.

Page 134: Feixa, C., Pereira, I., & Juris, J. (2009). Global citizenship and the 'new, new' social movements: Iberian connections. *Young 17*, 421.

Pages 135–6: Culture jamming, retrieved January 2010 from www.stayfreemagazine.org/9/adbusters.htm.

Page 137: Feixa, C., Pereira, I., & Juris, J. (2009). Global citizenship and the 'new, new' social movements: Iberian connections. *Young 17*, 421.

Page 141: CEA Agenda for Youth, 2007: 1. Canadian Education Association.

Index